The Little Black Book for Champions
Master Your Mindset from A to Z

Gene Morrow & Stefani Morrow

The Little Black Book for Champions
Copyright © 2016 by Transformation Living Systems

All rights reserved. No part of this book may be reproduced or transmitted in any form or by any means without written permission from the author.

ISBN ISBN-10:0990991113
ISBN-13:978-0-9909911-1-3

Printed in USA by CreateSpace Independent Publishing Platform

Dedication

The Little Black Book for Champions is dedicated to anyone who has the courage to ask for what they really want in life and the commitment to master the mindset that will manifest it.

Table of Contents

Foreword 7
Introduction 11
Altruism 15
Belief 19
Courage 24
Decision 30
Expectation 34
Fortitude 40
Growth 45
Honor 53
Impression 57
Joy 63
Knowledge 67
Legacy 70
Momentum 75
Now 80
Opportunity 85
Passion 89
Quieten 94
Resilience 98
Surrender 102
Thoughts 106
Universe 111
Vision 116
Words 121
X-ray 125
Yes 130
Zeal 135
Conclusion 139
References 149

Foreword

I believe, like you, that we were all created to do something and to be something. That something is significant to our families, our children, our businesses, our communities, and to the world. Greatness is not just our destination, it is our birthright. And the journey towards it begins with a calling and a willingness to face and overcome the impossible.

Even when we have to do it before and unlike anyone else.

When I met Gene and Stefani Morrow late last spring, I knew there was something exceptionally special about them. Over the course of a few months, we shared conversation after conversation about their lives, their experiences, and their vision for not only themselves, but for the people they felt most called to serve. The more we spoke, the clearer their purpose became to me.

The Morrows are here to transform people into the most powerful, the most purposeful, and the most profitable versions of themselves.

Through their conversation and commitment, I realized, among many things, that they were meant to help people to gain a deeper understanding about themselves and what they were capable of achieving in this life. Some of the most openhearted and transparent people I've ever met, they were willing, without hesitation, pride, or fear, to share the lessons they'd learned, to give it all, and to uncover the power and to embrace the process to push beyond logic and limitations.

But beyond that, Gene and Stefanie understand—undeniably—what it takes to be a champion.

Our work together has revealed to me that, unlike other business and success coaches, they weren't just beating the profit drum. Instead, they are going much further. They are moving people into a different, a deeper, conversation around what it means to really be successful. They are moving people beyond just driving bigger cars, owning fabulous homes, and making lots of money.

They are moving people into the mindset and behavior of true champions.

This is so fundamentally important because it takes more than an idea, a business plan, or even faith to win consistently. A champion is the totality—the essence—of who we are. It is our heart, mind, and soul. It is intellectual, emotional, and spiritual. And to be a champion in this life, we have to examine and embody all three elements.

First, a champion thinks. As you embark on this life-changing journey, I want you to assess your environment. Do an experiential audit of your life and study new strategies to achieve what you desire. Learn from the mistakes. Evaluate the losses. Take notes of the wins. It is the sum of these things that make you who you are and will ultimately propel you to where you want to be.

Emotionally, champions understand what drives them. It's what wills you to get up when you face those seemingly insurmountable, unyielding mountains in life. What fills your emotional reserve when the tank is running low? When you are in the fight of and for your life, you have to harness that belief, that commitment, that love to bring you through to the other side. Seek and discover that. If you are wondering what that is, allow me to give you a hint.

You rise when you understand that where you are—right now—is so much bigger than you.

True champions aren't just in it for them. They are always pursuing, leaping, and striving because of someone else. LeBron James didn't have to leave Miami and return to Cleveland as the unsung hero for himself—he did because, to him, the people of Cleveland deserved a championship. Another epic athlete, Michael Jordan, was driven to dominate the game not for himself, but for the people of Chicago.

As a champion, you are lifted not by the feeling you get when you win, but rather when we win.

The spiritual component of being a champion lies with our calling. Anyone can be successful at something they set out to do. But a champion feels—and knows—that they are called to that thing. This is what transcended the greats, like Muhammad Ali, beyond a few knock-outs and a belt. The victory was non-negotiable. Every fight was an epic battle and at the end of his career, he would be the only one standing at the top. He would not be denied greatness.

And neither should you.

This shift in thinking, doing, and being is what will transcend you beyond the surface level of success and into championship.

With this book, Gene and Stefani Morrow have proven that they understand every aspect of what it means to be a champion. And they have unlocked the secrets to the world champion in you. This is your Day 1.

I encourage you to devour these pages, to put these principles into action right now, and make the decision to work intimately with Transformation Living Systems to become the most powerful, most profitable version of yourself.

Go be who you are called to be and rise to level of that calling.

Go seize this magnificent moment in time to do something no one else has ever done.

Go be a champion.

Trevor Otts
Peak Performers Institute

Introduction

We were born to be champions.

The desire to achieve, to perform at the highest possible level—to win—is an innate part of who we are. It is, undeniably, what we were created to do. You, friend, are here to dominate everything you touch. So, if winning is in our DNA, why do we often feel like we're losing in the game of life?

Because, too often, we don't play to win.

We've all met someone who has beat the odds. This person may have overcome seemingly insurmountable obstacles. They may have stared death in the face, hit rock bottom and lost it all, or faced some of life's most harrowing circumstances. And they lived through it—not just to tell the story, but they actually thrived in the midst of it all. They refused to give up, to call it quits, or to allow life to drag them down and out.

So we cry tears of joy with them. We celebrate alongside them. We applaud them, admire them, and adore them.

Yet, deep down inside, we're wondering, how did they do that? What are they doing that I can't?

Here's the simplest truth:

They chose defiance over defeat. They decided to not allow what happened to them to be the end of the story.

They decided to stay in the game.

It is impossible to win in any area of life while sitting on the sidelines or hanging out in the bleachers. Living as a champion demands getting in the game. Right now, your circumstances, limiting beliefs, what others think and feel about you have you paralyzed in fear. You may be doubting yourself, questioning if you're smart enough, strong enough, or talented enough. Instead of propelling your life forward, you're cemented in indecision. And it's this mentality that keeps you on the edge of the arena, and in your life, instead of in the center of it. But it's in the center that you conquer. It's in the center where you thrive. The center is where you become a champion.

Will you decide to win just by stepping inside?

Winning begins with a mindset and a daily decision to get in the ring—even when things get hectic. Devastation, disappointment, and downturns will come and we can't control it. But we can govern our response. We can always choose to bounce back. We can always choose to maintain a positive perspective. And we can always choose to keep trying. Because, if we do, eventually, we will win.

Did you forget that you were winning before you set foot on this earth? You beat the odds to get there, to claim your spot, and you've been fighting to keep it ever since. You were supposed to be here. You were divinely created. Masterfully made. Let that sink down into your spirit. Claim it. Know it. Believe it.

We wrote The Little Black Book for Champions to help the fighter in you to regain focus and clarity of purpose. We've studied the behavior, the mindset, and the success of champions around the world and determined what makes them tick. We wanted to connect the dots, to determine the ties that bound these extraordinary people together. From athletes to world-renowned scholars, this book gives you twenty-six habits and principles they all share. The findings may surprise you. Keep reading to find out.

One trait that all champions have in common is a power voice. It is an internal message center, one that is filled with courage, confidence, and conviction. That voice is unwavering and speaks with authority and precision.

Our desire is that the words and principles in these pages will help you, most of all, to discover your power voice. Whether you are looking to improve your health, mend broken relationships, realize a more rewarding line of work, or discover what you are here on this earth to do, adopting these premises and principles as part of your mental landscape and thought processes will be paramount in your transformation.

Your success is waiting for you on the other side of your fears. Your destiny is beckoning you—calling you—to step forth into it. You were born and bred to conquer. You were created to be a champion. All you have to do is step into it.

Mindset Masters,

Altruism

noun al·tru·ism | principle or practice of unselfish concern for or devotion to the welfare of others

"*Good character consists of recognizing the selfishness that inheres in each of us and trying to balance it against the altruism to which we should all aspire. It is a difficult balance to strike, but no definition of goodness can be complete without it.*"

Alan Dershowitz

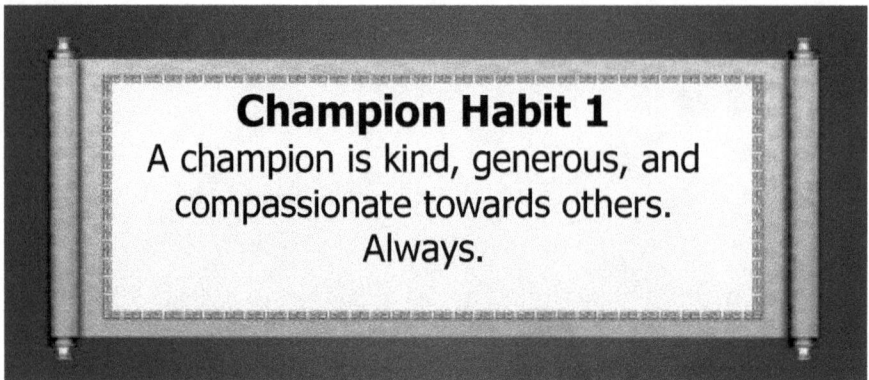

Altruism —including kindness, generosity, and compassion—are keys to a winning spirit and essential to our happiness. Research proves that acts of kindness, especially when they are spontaneous and out-of-the ordinary, can boost pleasure and overall productivity in the person doing the good deed.

Giving of yourself should come from an unselfish concern for other people. It involves doing things simply out of a desire to help, not an obligation of duty, loyalty, or religion. True altruism is when we willingly choose to promote someone else's welfare, even at a risk or cost to ourselves.

Everyday life is filled with opportunities to do something good for someone else—we see it all around us. There's the guy at the grocery store who kindly holds the door open as you rush in from the parking lot. The woman who gives twenty dollars to a homeless man, and the firefighter who routinely races into a burning building to save a complete stranger without giving it a second thought. What about the mom who always gives the last morsel of food to her children while she goes hungry? It's the sacrifice in these acts of kindness that make them so significant.

Though some believe that humans are fundamentally self-interested, recent research suggests otherwise. Studies have found that most people's first impulse is to cooperate rather than compete, and even toddlers spontaneously help people in need out of a genuine concern for their welfare. The most non-human primates display altruism—it's a basic function and natural instinct.

Often, we are so enveloped in our personal struggles that the thought of focusing on something or someone other than ourselves seems impossible and even counterintuitive. The reality is that giving is always better than receiving. In a culture marred by self-promotion and self-interest, sometimes living a life in which altruism is a mainstay is not a very convenient choice. But here are some reasons why generosity and kindness are a necessary and an integral part of the psyche of all champions:

- You'll feel better about yourself and everyone else. When you do something amazing for someone else, it raises your perception of yourself and everyone around you. You will begin to notice the beauty in the world and in other people. You'll smile more. You'll be more grateful for what you have and more aware of your gifts and talents. Kindness just make us feel good.

- It binds us together. Kindness fosters community and connection. Being benevolent to others is so natural to us, and kindness becomes a vibration and energy that draws other people in. Let a wave of humanity start with you.

- It sets the world on fire. Try this little experiment for yourself—make someone's day and observe them for a bit. More than likely, they will be inspired to pay it forward and be a blessing to someone else. Generosity is a chain reaction. Positivity is too. People love to be a part of something good; they just need a reason. Be the first and let the world follow.

You may feel that you don't enough to give—money, time, or even your heart. But decide to light the path for others in some way on your personal journey to excellence. Acts of service don't have to be obligatory or overwhelming. Focus on the little things that can make a meaningful difference in someone's life today. Can you hold that door or pick up the phone and call someone who needs to hear a cheerful voice? One unselfish act of service could change your life and the lives of countless others forever. When you give unselfishly, your life will be enriched in unimaginable ways.

When you give unselfishly, your life will be enriched in unimaginable ways.

Giving is living!

Belief

noun be·lief \an opinion or conviction: confidence in the truth or existence of something not immediately susceptible to rigorous proof

"Keep your dreams alive. Understand to achieve anything requires faith and belief in yourself, vision, hard work, determination, and dedication. Remember all things are possible for those who believe."

Gail Devers

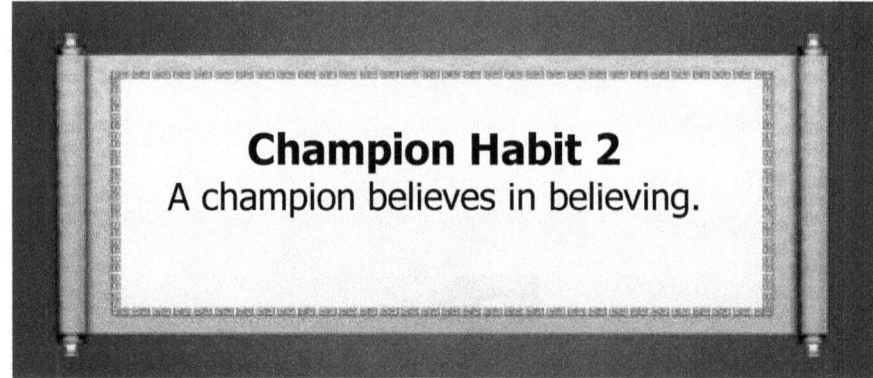

Champion Habit 2
A champion believes in believing.

Our personal beliefs are a combination of our mindset and makeup, including our dominant thoughts, upbringing, environment, and education. Our day-to-day lives, from the news we watch on television to the tidbits of celebrity gossip we consume on social media, continue to reinforce, or sometimes challenge, what we already believe. Every experience our mind encounters influences and helps to construct our belief system.

We each have our own unique belief system, which is similar to a filter that new information passes through before it comes into our awareness. Our beliefs are extremely complex. They are a sum of all the things we've learned throughout our entire lives. How we see ourselves, our capabilities, and even others is rooted in what we've been taught and accept as true. Our beliefs determine how we think the world works and embody the truths we hold to be self-evident and accept without question. So to make any new data or input meaningful in our minds, we always compare it to our existing belief system. At times, those beliefs serve us well. All too often, however, they do not.

Our beliefs will always make perfect sense to us – at least until we are troubled by something in our lives and begin to re-evaluate them. When our lives aren't yielding the results we want—we're unhappy, unsatisfied, disappointed, or restless—we look inward and begin to question whether our circumstances demand change. And that change often begins with our beliefs.

The good news is that you can shift. If you find your belief system needs an overhaul, know there is always the option to hit the reset button.

The first step is to evaluate what you believe. There are some key questions to start with as you begin to truly evaluate your personal belief system:

- What do I believe?
- What has impacted or shaped my beliefs?
- Are these truly my beliefs or have I taken on the beliefs of others?
- Which of my beliefs are based in love? What about fear? Anger?

Understanding that your belief system is real and intact is necessary to really to win at anything in life. Nothing significant can be accomplished without a sound and unwavering sense of belief. You have to believe in something or you'll fall for anything. It is your belief that guides your integrity and character. It is your belief that will keep you upright and steadfast when life's inevitable challenges threaten to overtake and overwhelm you. It is your belief that gives you strength and endurance beyond what you thought you were capable of.

> *It is your belief that gives you strength and endurance beyond what you thought you were capable of.*

You become what you think you are and the world becomes what you think it is. How do you see the world? How do you see yourself in it? How do you view your relationships with people?

It is not easy to change your way of looking at things. However, there is absolutely a way to build a more productive belief system that best serves your greater good. Once you've taken an account of what you believe and why, it's time to clean house. Clear the clutter from your mind and replace that negativity with a more positive, champion-fueled mindset.

Here's how to start:

1. Assess your entire belief system again and determine which beliefs are serving you well and which ones are not working for you.
2. Identify the beliefs that are getting in the way of your major goals.
3. Decide what your overall perspective is going to be. Do you want to have a positive outlook or a pessimistic, cynical one? (You get to choose.)

Pull your beliefs out one at a time and deeply evaluate them. By embracing the ones you want to keep, you make them stronger. Look for irrational beliefs. Freely eradicate the ones that have been constructed from erroneous teachings and partial truths. Challenge the beliefs that don't give you good results, the ones that have negative emotions attached, or those that seem to produce unsatisfactory outcomes. Continue to engage in this discovery process in all areas of your life, and commit to it for as long as it takes to create beliefs that are fully aligned with your life's purpose.

Your new, fortified belief system is not only magnanimous—it's magnetic. As you step out into the world with a clear sense of who you are and what you stand for, you will begin to attract like-minded individuals. You will create the conditions necessary for your goals and dreams to manifest on a material plane.

Your beliefs should never go down without a fight. Stand for what's yours. You must continue to believe when naysayers, dream-busters, and hope-snatchers appear to have a louder voice, a wider audience, and a greater sphere of influence. You must believe in your ability to produce the life you desire and deserve in times of feast and in times of famine.

Your beliefs should never go down without a fight.

Don't ever stop believing!

Courage

noun cour·age | the quality of mind or spirit that enables a person to face difficulty, danger, or pain without fear; bravery

"I learned that courage was not the absence of fear, but the triumph over it. The brave man is not he who does not feel afraid, but he who conquers that fear."

Nelson Mandela

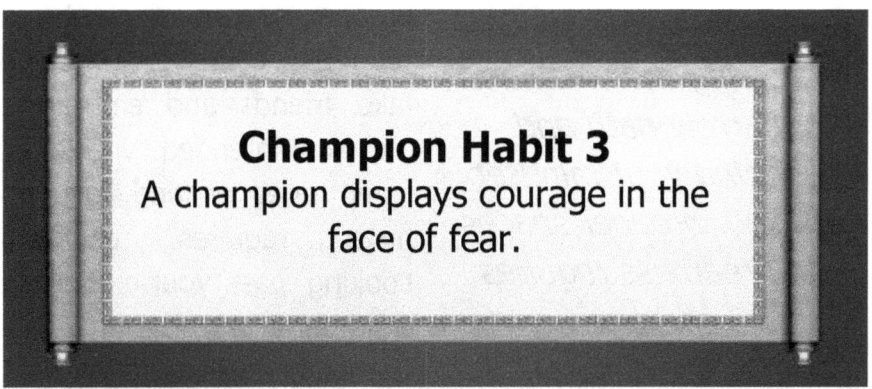

Champion Habit 3
A champion displays courage in the face of fear.

Courage is considered, by many, to be one of the most important foundations of humanity. In a world where conformity is often celebrated and presented to the masses as the norm, it takes courage to wade out into the deep waters of your destiny. Because so many people fear rejection and embrace mediocrity, playing by the rules and following the crowd is a much more appealing reality. This explains why the notion of living a life without any real limits seems to be a remote figment of the imagination—at least for most. But for the person who desires a new sense of normal, a limitless life is not merely a possibility.

> *In a world where conformity is often celebrated and presented to the masses as the norm, it takes courage to wade out into the deep waters of your destiny.*

It is the only option.

Courage is required to play and, ultimately, to win at the game of life. Trying your hand at something new and seeking what fits you will require courage. Rejecting the small and narrow path and opening your mindset to new,

> *Rejecting the small and narrow path and opening your mindset to new, broader spaces of greatness requires courage.*

broader spaces of greatness requires courage. Ditching fake friends and embracing the well-intended village of loved ones waiting for you have requires courage. Looking past your perceived limitations and creating life-changing opportunities calls for courage.

And so does transforming your dreams into realities.

Willfully subjecting yourself to scorn, ridicule, and the possibility of failure to follow a dream will demand your absolute courage and boldness. The presence of courage does not equate to the absence of fear. It simply means acting in spite of fear.

It's critical for each of us to detach from fear and tap into our courage to live our dreams. Happiness can only occur if we are living our life in a way that is congruent with our authentic selves, and authenticity requires that we be brave enough to embrace who we are and who we were called to be. Consider these courageous steps that you can take today to finally launch your dream:

See it: First, make your dream real by giving it power and presence in your life. What is on your heart to do? Pen your memoir and become a bestselling author? Experience a South African safari? Start an online business? If nothing comes to mind immediately, what has your spirit been speaking you about that you've suppressed? Yes, that thing. Pull that out. There is no dream to large or too small.

Strategize it: Every dream needs a blueprint. You have a vision in your mind, now how are you going to get there? What skills do you need? How much money or time? What about people? These are the questions you'll need to ask yourself and answer. Pull out a fresh notebook and lay it all out. Seek out someone either online or in your city who may have done something similar and reach out to them. Ask if they'd be willing to chat over coffee or hop on Skype and answer a few questions. If the meeting goes well, you may even consider asking the person to mentor you for six to twelve months to get your dream idea off of the group. Don't be afraid to ask for help and don't get stuck in creating a plan from scratch. Follow a roadmap that's already been defined. You just need to get to the final destination.

Share it: Hold yourself accountable by telling somebody about your dream. Choose someone who will protect your sacred vision, not the friend who is negative and lacking an open mind. Find at least one dream partner and discuss your ideas and plans with them. Be willing to do the same with them. The constant exchange of support will do you a world of good.

Silence it: As your vision begins to take shape, beware of the doubtful thoughts that will creep in. You'll hear things like, "I don't have what it takes," or "This is too hard. I should give up now." Shut it down! Replace those fear-filled words with new, fortifying ones. "I got this!" is a great start. Remind yourself daily of how powerful and brave you are. Eventually, it will become second nature to you.

Learning to center your mind, body, and spirit with a few minutes of deep breathing and meditation can have tremendous benefits in the absence of courage. Use and practice the following affirmations to strengthen your courage each day:

1. I will share my gifts freely and without reservation or hesitation as I feel called to do so.

2. I understand I am here for a reason and a purpose.

3. I love myself enough to protect my dreams from naysayers and doubters. I will seek positive people to surround myself with.

4. I will not allow fear to kill my dreams.

5. I will speak up when I feel physically or emotionally threatened or unsafe.

6. I refuse to allow others to make my question myself and my worth.

7. I will give love and receive love as abundantly as possible.

8. I release the pain of the past. Any guilt, any shame, any brokenness, and any insecurity is now healed.

9. I will be open—in my heart, mind, and spirit.

10. I welcome new people, experiences, and ideas with outstretched arms.

There will be times when you are the only courageous soul in a room overflowing with cowards who are too afraid to take a chance on themselves or have an opinion contrary to the masses. Get comfortable with that. Choose courage today and each day that follows—even when you are the only one feeling bold and brave. While it may appear to be the unpopular choice today, the dividends that courage will pay in your future are unending. Each day you will be presented with an opportunity to succumb to conformity, to take on complacency, to give in to the status quo, and to comply with limited thinking. Choice is one of your greatest assets and is always with you. Always live in integrity and choose wisely.

> *There will be times when you are the only courageous soul in a room overflowing with cowards who are too afraid to take a chance on themselves or have an opinion contrary to the masses. Get comfortable with that.*

Be courageous!

Decision

noun de·ci·sion | something that is decided: resolution. the act of or need for making up one's mind

"If you choose not to decide, you still have made a choice."

Neil Peart

The Little Black Book for Champions

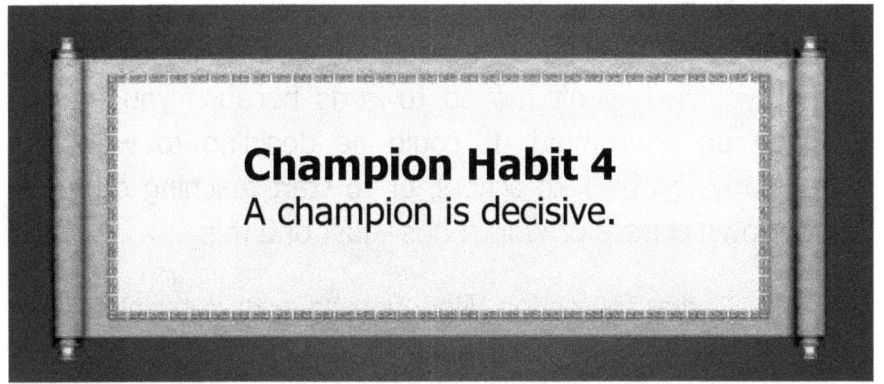

Champion Habit 4
A champion is decisive.

Your future is shaped by the decisions you are making, or are not making, right now. Your tomorrow rests in the hands of your choices, and the life you lead today is a result of the decisions you made in the past. But you can completely shift the trajectory of your life, if you're willing.

Do you have areas in your life that are stalled because a decision needs to be made? Have you been postponing making that decision? Did you throw your hands in the air and give up too soon on any of your goals because your decision didn't produce the result you were looking for the first time? Now would probably be an excellent time to put all of that in the past. Why not start today?

Deciding to do something differently—be it to think, act, or both—is often the hardest step in achieving your goals and going after your dreams. If you have been avoiding the decision making process, commit to breaking through that barrier right here and now.

Here is a mini experiment that will help you to begin making decisions more readily and confidently:

Narrow your focus: Decisiveness is a muscle that needs to be built. So start small and slow. Choose one goal that you've haven't moved towards because you haven't made up your mind. It could be deciding to work out regularly, go back to school, or to start teaching others in your own classes or workshops—just one thing.

Define the action. Now you have to determine what it will take to reach your goal. Grab a clean sheet of paper and list four ways to take action. For example, if your desire is to teach, possible action steps may include offering to lead a class on someone else's platform or creating your own.

Weigh the pros and cons of each choice. You don't need to stress yourself over this process—trust your instinct and allow your heart to lead you to the right one. Don't allow the lure of laziness to get you; choosing the easy route may be quick and require the least effort, but may not be best. Which option will give you most lasting, most substantive result? Choose that one. Don't cheat yourself.

Back it up: You now know what you want to do and how you need to get there. So the next step is to commit. Tomorrow, get up and move! Get started and take action. At the end of five days, assess your progress and adjust as needed. Remember, the entire journey may not be clear, and that's okay. The important part is to just keep moving.

Congratulations, you have just taken control of your life! The more you practice making decisions and following through on them, the more skilled you will become at it and the easier it will be for you. Every decision you make will move you in the direction you want to go, provided that you make a total commitment and take consistent action. Be decisive and flex your decision-making muscles often.

*Be decisive and flex your
decision-making muscles often.*

Expectation

noun ex·pec·ta·tion | the act or state of looking forward or anticipating

"We see what we ASSUME we will see. If you believe the world is evil, you will see evil. If you believe the world is good, you will see good. To change how life looks, change how you see life - change your expectations of life."

Jonathan Lockwood Huie

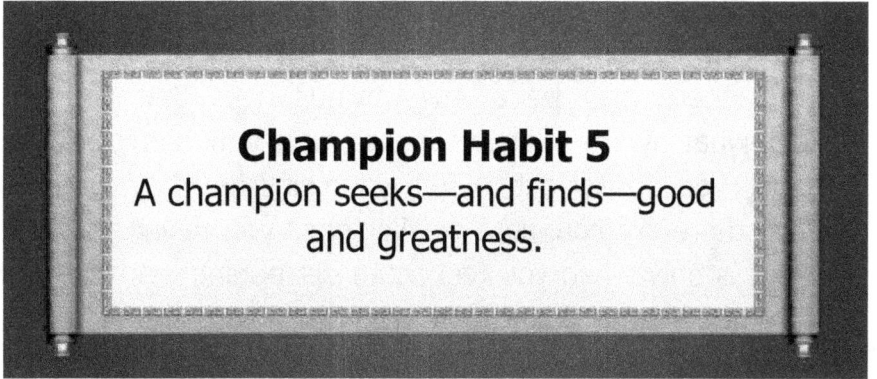

Champion Habit 5
A champion seeks—and finds—good and greatness.

You may not realize it but your expectations, or lack thereof, may be undermining your efforts to win in life. A lack of expectancy plagues you and contaminates your thoughts, causing you to be irritable, disappointed, and disillusioned. When you have expectations of others and they aren't met, you lash out with unkind words, act irrationally, or make poor decisions. Poor expectations are so insidious that you will clamor to maintain them even after you have clear evidence that they are unfounded.

Expectations show up in many forms—from what we expect of ourselves to what others expect of us and what we expect of them. You may have high, low, or even negative expectations. You also have large expectations and thousands of small expectations that arise in your life every day. Your expectations have their own unique expression but are typically similar to what every other human desires in this world. So you are not alone. But as you learn to free yourself from the burden of expectations, you can start to eliminate them and refuse to allow them to define your daily experience. When they're negative, expectations hurt us and keep us bound to lives that in no way reflect the people we desire to be.

It is so amazing that despite the suffering caused by your expectations, you hardly notice them most of the time. Sure, there may be a few obvious ones that you are somewhat aware of, but even so, you only sort of notice them; you do not act to free yourself from their tyranny. Plus, there are countless smaller ones you never notice at all. It is only when you feel acute disappointment that you become aware. When you get hurt, you are suddenly conscious that you've become possessed by your expectations. But those moments are just reminders—small pricks on your spirit that eventually become big wounds. For every time we've been failed, we've experienced many hours of dissatisfaction, impatience, and tension that you never realized arose from what you thought should happen as opposed to what actually did.

The beauty is you do not have to continue to suffer from the stronghold of disappointment. It is one of the most troublesome areas of life, yet it's one that can be changed. Even a little effort makes a huge difference. But first you must penetrate the nature of your expectations, observe how they manifest themselves in your life, and access another way of approaching the future.

If you want to truly shift in this area, it is critical for you to understand the difference between expectations and possibilities. Expectations assume a certain result and are future- based. They actually narrow your options, retard your imagination, and blind you to opportunities. They create pressure in your life and hold your present sense of well-being hostage to a future that may or may not happen. Expectations create rigidity in your life and cause you to react impulsively to any perceived threat to the future that you believe you deserve.

When you are controlled by your expectations, you are living a contingent life; you cannot be free in the present moment. You cannot be happy with a beautiful sunset because the weatherwoman predicted rain later in the week. A moment of warmth between you and another is weighed by wondering if this is the one. You remain anchored to a mediocre today because you're too busy analyzing what could happen tomorrow. Every experience is interpreted in the context of an expected future instead of living for and in the now.

Can you see how enslaving this perspective is to you? If you could control the future, perhaps this mindset would be beneficial to you, but is that the case? Likely not. To deny the truth—the present moment—of life is a fool's errand and is costly to your well-being.

In contrast to expectations, possibilities are based in the present moment, where you're alive to the mystery of life. You live as fully as you can in the present based on your values, which reflect your preferences for the future. You do not assume the future will come to pass. To the contrary, you realize that the future is unknown so you simply revel in the moment, in the here and now. Being open to possibilities

> *Until you are enlightened, you will repeatedly fall into expectations instead of leaning into possibilities.*

acknowledges that what you may think you want changes with time, or that there is another possibility could bring you equal or more happiness. Real joy, then, is that which is available to you right now.

This ability to respond to life rather than react to it is the primary distinction between champions and underachievers who are caught in the suffering of their existence. You may often find yourself reacting to the behavior of others or to changes in your circumstances and never realize it is a result of expecting others or your life to be a certain way. When you respond this way, when you refuse to be free, or allow yourself to be happy, you are choosing expectation over possibility.

Imagine the freedom that comes from responding to life's shifts and changes rather than reacting to them.

It doesn't mean that you won't unconsciously create expectations over and over again (no one is expecting you to be perfect which in itself is just another expectation). Until you are enlightened, you will repeatedly fall into expectations instead of exploring into possibilities.

Learn to live an existence filled with possibilities rather than expectations.

Becoming mindfully aware of expectations—and compassionate with yourself when you feel yourself caught in them—is necessary. Repeating this exercise in your life will develop the skill to completely release yourself from expectations. Even when expectations threaten to creep in, you won't be controlled by them.

Learn to live an existence filled with possibilities rather than expectations.

Fortitude

noun for·ti·tude | strength and firmness of mind; resolute endurance

"I know of no higher fortitude than stubbornness in the face of overwhelming odds."

Louis Nizer

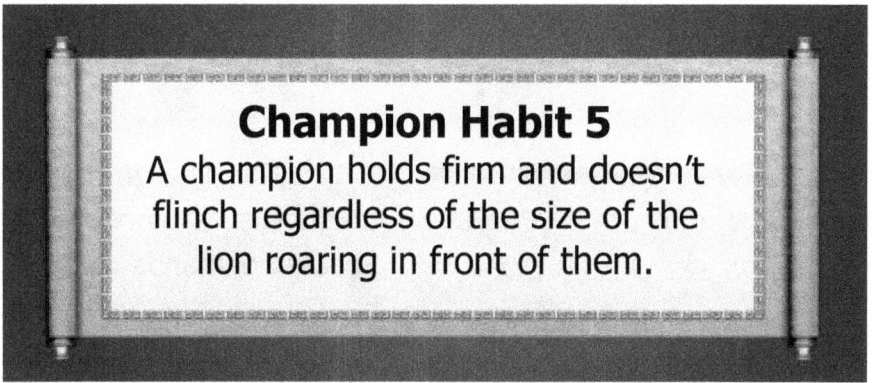

Champion Habit 5
A champion holds firm and doesn't flinch regardless of the size of the lion roaring in front of them.

We've all seen it. The collegiate athlete who has all of the promise the world has to offer. They rule the field or the court. Agents and coaches from all over the country—sometimes the world—are putting in their bids, hoping to be chosen. This kid has magic. This is the first-round draft pick headed straight for the promise of the pros. The deal gets signed. Everyone is waiting with baited breath to watch a new star rise.

But once they get there, they flop.

An athlete may have great athletic ability, yet they could not cut it at the professional level. Others might be less talented with the ball, get picked late in the draft, and go onto become super stars. How is this possible? What distinguishes the two? What could be more important than physical ability?

The answer is simple: mental toughness.

Mental toughness is what separates the champion from the merely good. It separates the musicians that play small party gigs from the rock stars who fill stadiums. Someone without mental toughness can have all the natural talents or ability in the world and not make it as far as someone with the mentality of a champion and average ability.

> *You can do whatever you set out to do— if you make up your mind that it's achievable.*

The key to mental toughness is consistency. Success demands that you be consistently motivated, maintain a positive attitude, control your emotions, and remain calm under fire. When your mind is right and strong, you are energetic and ready for action. If you apply these ideals day in and day out, if you embody and embrace them, you will reach new heights in whatever endeavors you seek. You will play that sport or musical instrument. You will build a robot or write that novel. You can do whatever you set out to do— if you make up your mind that it's achievable.

Let's examine the traits of mental toughness:

Be willing to stand alone. Collaboration has its purpose and place, but, sometimes—most times—you have to walk and live it out by yourself. Learn how to push yourself and find what motivates you from the inside out. Think about a time when you flopped. Allow that to push you to never repeat it. Conversely, call to memory that moment when you flew. Keep that close to you too and get familiar with the feeling of winning. And celebrate your wins. Be your own cheering squad.

Be positive. We typically spend too much time focused on what we can't do as opposed to what we can.

Don't dwell in your weaknesses or what you're lacking; instead, play up your strengths. Are you a so-so writer but a phenomenal speaker? Great—speak whenever you can. Your gifts are just as powerful as the next person's. Own those.

Be calm. Practice emotional steadiness in high-pressure situations. Keep your cool and don't allow other people to penetrate your thoughts or derail you. Focus on the prize, the end game. Circumstances will change. Obstacles will come. Loved ones will leave. These things are life, not stop signs. Dust yourself off and keep going.

Be ready. Preparation is key. There will come a time when everything you've learned and planned for will come together and it will be time to show and prove. Stay in constant state of preparation so you'll be ready to step up at a moment's notice. Even if everything is not perfect when opportunity knocks, answer the door anyway. It's okay to figure things out as you go.

The great thing about mental toughness is that you are not born with it. You don't have to learn it at a young age. Mental toughness comes simply from the decision to show up consistently and do the work. You can start today and reach levels of your game, relationships, and success that you never thought possible. Outstanding athletic prowess, superior talent, or business intellect can only take you so far.

> *Mental toughness comes simply from the decision to show up consistently and do the work.*

Without mental toughness, reaching your full potential will only be a dream. Toughen up today!

Growth

noun |the act, process, or manner of growing; development: gradual increase

"The only way that we can live is if we grow. The only way that we can grow is if we change. The only way that we can change is if we learn. The only way we can learn is if we are exposed. And the only way that we can become exposed is if we throw ourselves out into the open. Do it. Throw yourself."

C. JoyBell C.

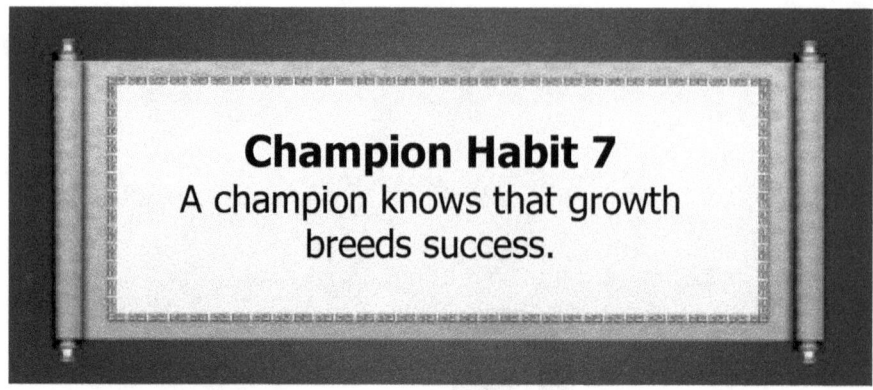

Champion Habit 7
A champion knows that growth breeds success.

Personal growth and development is a transformational process to improve your state of being. It could be physical, emotional, intellectual, spiritual, social, financial, or any combination of those. The common factor is that something is not up to par in your life and you realize you need to change it. So you seek the tools and resources to make it happen.

Growth is often triggered by an important life event that inspires you to be better and want more. Growth empowers and prompts you to seek, and find, where your full potential lies. The result is a more satisfying and meaningful life, which is evident in your relationships, career, self-belief, confidence, as well as your worldview.

You have to do more than want it; you have to go after it.

Dissatisfaction with life and the direction it's headed in is a catalyst for growth and development. To change course and create a satisfying life, you have to do more than want it; you have to go after it. And ultimately getting it is a process, a series of deliberate steps, to get from where you are to where you want to be.

Once you start moving, the results are endless. You will find meaning and purpose in yourself that was absent before. Life goals will become possible. You will leverage your full potential to benefit yourself and others. Unused skills and talents will be discovered. Old relationships will be strengthened and new ones will be easily formed. Your self-image and self-confidence will be boosted to new heights.

Every person is a unique and, as a result, a universal strategy for personal growth and development cannot exist. Everyone's pathway to progress is a personalized journey and it's up to you to decide which route to take and where it might lead.

Consider these questions to help guide you towards your own path:

- **What do I have in my toolbox?**

    Assess what you're phenomenal at and what skills you lack. Determine what areas, personally and professionally, that you excel in and where you struggle.

- **What do I want to change?**

    Examine what you want to improve about yourself and why it's important for you to change those characteristics. Understanding why change is important will increase the likelihood that you'll stick with your commitment to do something about it. Also, look at the habits of people who are successful in the areas you want to change. Are they sticklers for time? Highly productive? Do they exercise every day? Remember there is always a blueprint!

- **What do I need to seek out?**

Decide what new experiences, skills, and knowledge are necessary to become the person you desire to be and explore all opportunities available to you. Get out in to the world and discover what books, conferences, workshops, Meetups, and even places of worship that can help you to grow your mind, spirit, and social interactions.

- **How long will it take?**

List the steps you intend to take to get to the finish line. Refer back to the plan regularly to keep you on track.

Why are your growth and continued learning so important? Because it's an ongoing process of self-discovery and crucial to achieving success in every area of your life. Jim Rohn, known as America's foremost business philosopher, said it best:

> "You must constantly ask yourself these questions: Who am I around? What are they doing to me? What have they got me reading? What have they got me saying? Where do they have me going? What do they have me

thinking? And most important, what do they have me becoming? Then ask yourself the big question: Is that okay? Your life does not get better by chance; it gets better by change."

If you understand and accept that you are the average of the five people you spend the most time with, which is another philosophy established by Jim Rohn, what does this say about your character? What does this say about the direction of your life? The people you surround yourself with feed you, spiritually and mentally. They will either drive you or drown you—the decision is yours. So it's essential to guard your mind and be selective about who you allow to influence it.

> *The people you surround yourself with feed you, spiritually and mentally. They will either drive you or drown you—the decision is yours.*

The mind is a magical gift from God with unlimited potential for learning and creativity. It is the control center of your life, your compass, and determines whether you are constructive or destructive, optimistic or pessimistic, proactive or reactive.

Your mind is your greatest asset and must be constantly expanded with new ideas. If you continue to feed it positive, inspirational thoughts and information, your mind can provide you with the power and authority to design an amazing life, just as a painter would create a work of art.

There are a myriad of reasons why our personal growth is so important and vital to our success and fulfillment in all areas of life. Here are four reasons to commit to your personal growth today:

- Personal growth helps you to edge out the competition. If you stay sharp with your skills and expertise, you will be in position to choose opportunities as opposed to waiting be chosen. Whether you are an entrepreneur or climbing the career ladder, clients and employers alike are seeking the best people for the job. Also, growth and development

- Evolution is a constant and you want to stay in the mix. Those who don't actively seek growth become mentally and physically lazy and are lulled into the comfort of complacency. The world is constantly changing around us, so shift right along with it. When you are open to change, you'll adopt a more positive attitude to changing circumstances and challenges as they arise.

- The person who possesses the most confidence is the guaranteed champion. Growth is a direct link to the mindset of an overcomer. The more you know, the more likely you are to assert yourself as a leader and make success you're a requirement for living.

- Your feelings of self-worth elevate alongside your knowledge. The more you invest in developing your mind and spirit, the more life wins you'll acquire. Excellence makes us feel powerful and necessary in the world and that is a feeling you want to embrace and keep close.

So why not start your personal development right now? Here are a few, very practical options:

- Books: Never underestimate the power of reading. Spend some time in the personal development section of your local library or bookstore and comb through material that speaks to you. If you don't have time to read a book from cover to cover, audiobooks are a fantastic alternative. You can also find a host of ebooks (some are free) online.

- Experts: Find a speaker or coach who specializes in personal and professional development and seek out their content. Start with their websites, social media, and livestreams. If they are hosting an event in your city or nearby, plan to attend. You'd be surprised how inexpensive some conferences or workshops are. The motivational content and energy will do your mind and heart good. And you'll learn a lot along the way!

- Mentorship: Sometimes you need 1:1 time with someone to really grasp knowledge. If you identity an expert who you believe can help to take you to your next level, don't hesitate to reach out to them. Send a well-crafted email to request a coffee meeting to talk or offer to volunteer to serve in some capacity to get some face time. If the discussion goes well, speak up and ask for some opportunities to build a relationship. It never hurts to ask.

Your personal growth is your responsibility, not your employers, your spouse, or your friends. Grow your mind, grow yourself, and you will grow your life! After all, growth is the very essence of who we are as human beings, so don't allow yourself to become stagnant. Keep evolving—always.

Honor

noun hon·or \honesty, fairness, or integrity in one's beliefs and actions.

"The greatest way to live with honor in this world is to be what we pretend to be."

Socrates

Champion Habit 8
Champions live in integrity.

The phrase "Honor Your Word," in its simplest context, means you will do what you say you will do.

When you honor your word, the most important action is the doing. Did you do what you said you would do, when you said you would do it? The doing is about living up your commitment. You should always try to keep your word. Champions live in integrity and always honor their word!

To choose to not honor your word is to choose not to have integrity in your life.

It is not always possible to keep your word, but it is always possible to honor it. If circumstances arise and it's not possible to keep your word, inform all parties involved and attend to any issues that may arise as a result of your inability to keep your word. When this is done, you are honoring word despite not having kept it and you have maintained your integrity. To choose to not honor your word is to choose not to have integrity in your life.

It is the most noble pursuit of humanity to become as whole and complete has a human being can be. This endeavor includes the pursuit of wisdom, living a life of love and compassion, and taking an active role in creating a world that works for everyone—a world in in which all can be honored. If that is not your pursuit, then what is the point?

When we live our lives with honor and integrity, it means that we let our actions speak for who we are and what we believe in. Integrity is a choice we make, and it's a choice we must keep making, over and over again.

Here are some reasons why living with honor and integrity are so important:

Reason #1: When we are led our integrity, we don't have to worry about whether we are doing right or wrong. Integrity gives us a sense of peace and freedom since there's nothing to hide. You are not lying, stealing, or cheating anyone. Your intention is good. You'll sleep better at night.

Reason #2: Integrity builds respect and trust. If someone can believe that you are honest and trustworthy, the relationship can blossom. Mates and friends can trust you with their emotions; clients and business partners and associates can trust you with their money and ideas. Trust opens doors of opportunity in every area of our lives.

Reason #3: People want to be like good people. As your integrity elevates you to the status of leadership, others will look up to you and naturally model your behavior. Set a shining example for them and stay upright in your actions and your words. Honor is a hallmark of leadership.

If you are not a person of honor and integrity, then how valuable are you as a parent, sibling, friend, employee, employer, or spouse? If you've never been tested in terms of your integrity and character, keep living. Just know when that day comes you have a choice to respond with honor.

Impression

noun im·pres·sion \the first and immediate effect of an experience or perception upon the mind; sensation; an image in the mind caused by something external to it; a strong effect produced on the intellect, feelings, or conscience.

"A thousand words will not leave so deep an impression as one deed."

Henrik Ibsen

Champion Habit 9
A champion leaves a mark.

First impressions, while brief, are famously hard to change and will likely color your relationship with the other person for years to come. Do you convey confidence? Self-assurance? Authenticity? When people talk to you they instantly judge you and decide whether or not you're someone worth knowing. Due to this natural inclination, you need to always leave a solid first impression. You never know if it may lead to a new, amazing friend or open a door to an opportunity you've been waiting for.

Remember that approaching random people to converse and get to know them is an invaluable skill to have. Not only does it expand your social circle, it makes you more comfortable with social interaction in general. If you're able to strike up a legitimate conversation with someone you don't know, imagine how amazing you'd feel when talking to someone you're already familiar with?

When you meet someone, there are things you should always take into account, such as the context of the meeting (personal or business) and what that person is doing at the moment of initiation. Tweak your approaches based on these two things. For example, when you are in a more casual and personal setting, you probably don't want to be as formal as you would with a new potential employer. Also, you never want to make someone stop everything they're doing just to speak to you if you've never met them before. It's rude, and no one likes to be interrupted.

If you struggle in this area, here are some behaviors to put into immediate practice that all champions know and do to leave a lasting impression:

Display Confidence

Confidence is contagious—and noticeable. When you are headed out to a social or networking event, a big meeting, or even a presentation, take some time to relax, take a few deep breaths and shake off any stress before you walk into the space.

Practice your greeting and smile in the mirror. Have a powerful introduction in mind to tell people who you are and what you do. Look people in the eye when speaking to them. Watch your posture and body language. All of these things make you appear more confident.

Make Your Appearance Memorable

Your clothing, hair, and even your accessories make a statement about you. Think about the image you want to convey. Are you a creative? Button-up professional? A mix of the two? Dress the part. Add personality to your appearance with colorful pocket squares or fun eyewear. If high heels are a part of your look, wear them all the time. People will soon begin to associate you with those things.

Be an Interesting Person

Your conversation with others is so important. Be able to hold a genuine, interesting discussion with people you meet. Ask about them, what brings them to the event, what they do for a career, or where they grew up. Share similar details in exchange. Build authentic connections based on how you can help each other. Listen attentively and show you care.

We want to challenge you to start becoming more aware of the little first impressions you are making on people. Remember, these tiny impressions, when combined together, form your personal brand and ultimately influence every part of your life.

Make a list of the first impressions you are making on the people who are important in helping you achieve your goal. To give you a head start, here is a list of five.

1. The first email exchange. Carefully craft the first email you send to anyone, particularly a potential or new client or someone important. Check the tone, be sure it's clear and easy to follow, and catch those spelling and grammatical errors.

2. The first hello. Whether it's a date or a business dinner, your greeting counts. Be enthusiastic and alive. It speaks volumes about your interest. Make it obvious that you are interested in the person and wanting to get to know them.

3. The first conversation. Do you dominate the discussion or can you let the other person get a word in edgewise? Are you engaged and fully present or is your mind wandering? Is your phone put away so you can offer your full attention? Are you offensive? These are the things people will remember most.

4. The first challenge. When you are new to a situation, all eyes are on you, especially in times of crisis. Can you rise to the occasion and take control? Are you solution-oriented or do you shrink when the going gets tough? Do you lash out or can you speak softly and directly when needed? Keep your cool.

5. The first time someone interfaces with your business. Is your receptionist, staff, and even voicemail greeting an accurate reflection of your brand? It's the little things that count. If you are welcoming someone to your office, make sure your waiting and work areas are neat and clean. Remind greeters or anyone interacting with clients or customers to be friendly and upbeat.

Surely you could list so many more first impressions we make on people. Each of these little first imprints will play a defining role in everything from your relationships to your career. Start focusing on making your first impressions count, while at the same time becoming the person who is consistent with the reputation you are creating for yourself. As you strive to become the person you need to be to achieve your goals, you will begin to make many positive first impressions without even trying. They will become part of your standard operating procedure.

Don't ever allow yourself to think something doesn't matter. No action, gesture, or conversation is too small when it comes to how others perceive you.

Champions understand everything matters!

No action, gesture, or conversation is too small when it comes to how others perceive you.

Joy

noun |the emotion of great delight or happiness caused by something exceptionally good or satisfying; keen pleasure; elation.

"There are souls in this world who have the gift of finding joy everywhere and leaving it behind them when they go."

Faber

Champion Habit 10
A champion seeks and speaks joy.

Do you know anyone who cannot find fulfillment in anything, has no sense of real purpose, or has lost hope and is wallowing in bitterness and resentment? It can be a real chore to have joyless people in your life. In most cases these associations will begin to compromise your own happiness when left unaddressed and unchecked. A joyful, peaceful, and fulfilling life is your God-given birthright!

> *A joyful, peaceful, and fulfilling life is your God-given birthright!*

Living with joy is a perspective and choice that you must be willing to make daily. Despite your circumstances, you have control over your emotions and reactions. Of course, things happen in life that could leave even the strongest human being feeling cynical, depressed, untrusting, and downright broken. In these trying times, we must not let what is happening around us negatively impact what is within us—our decided joy.

Real joy can only be manifested in the present, that life-changing instant when we finally shed the past, let go of the future, and we are just there, abiding in that moment.

Brooding over what was and agonizing over what might be are wastes of energy that are sure to steal your joy, always. The most authentic expression of joy is appreciating and living in your now.

If your joy levels are solid, congrats! You are doing better than the masses. If you could use a boost in this department, here is a list of suggested ingredients that can activate and sustain more joy in your life starting now. Customize your recipe for joy by selecting elements that resonate with you the most and vowing to embody them daily:

- Create a happiness circle of people you love.
- Evolve constantly. Learn one new thing every day.
- Find the humor in life and laugh about something.
- Set aside a safe space of stillness, meditation, and peace in your home.
- Live life to the fullest.
- Commit to a wellness routine and practice physical, spiritual, and emotional self-care.
- Love people for who and what they are.
- Be willing to change when necessary.
- Seek out things that fulfill you.
- See your backyard. See your city. See the world.

- Escape in your mind and dream constantly.

- Notice the beauty in everything.

- Fill up on what makes you happiest, books, music, art, people you love. Never allow your happiness reservoir to run too low.

- Learn to love and appreciate yourself.

- Free your spirit from worry, guilt, and shame. Accept that you did your best. (Because it's true.)

Knowledge

noun knowl·edge \acquaintance with facts, truths, or principles, as from study or investigation.

"When you know a thing, to hold that you know it; and when you do not know a thing, to allow that you do not know it - this is knowledge."

Confucius

Champion Habit 11
Champions learn while living and apply while doing.

There is a common misconception circulating around these days. We have all heard it and have been guilty of declaring countless times. It the Latin phrase, "Scientia est Potestas" which means "Knowledge is Power." The well-known phrase was first coined by Sir Francis Bacon in 1597, and we continue to hear these words referenced in presentations, discussions, and heralded across platforms all over the world. But there's just one small caveat to this train of thought—possession of knowledge alone will not result in the presence of power. Knowledge is not power. Knowledge is certainly necessary, even critical. Knowledge is valuable and can even give us access to power. But no, knowledge is not power.

Action is power.

Here's a very surface level example: If you're sitting on the railroad tracks and a freight train is bearing down on you, it is not enough to know you should get off the tracks. Your survival instincts and thoughts of self-preservation, what

Action, not knowledge, is power.

you know, must translate into immediate action. Taking action is the only way to get off the tracks! Without action, knowledge is nothing.

Learning and education has been a dear friend of ours. We believe one of the most important investments a person can make is committing to their personal growth and development. However, once new learning is obtained, application must follow to support desired outcomes. Ignorance on fire is better than knowledge on ice! If the attainment of knowledge is never translated into action, what purpose has it truly served?

Knowledge (especially when it's technical and specialized) in an area may open a door for you, but your ability to be promoted, sustained, or even stand out among others in life or in business will always be the result of practical experience. You must use what you've learned and put it into action. What does the unschooled millionaire know that the college-educated taxi cab driver does not? One specialized in gaining knowledge and the other gained information and translated that data into massive action.

Knowledge is theory, but only through action can we produce real power evidenced in practice.

Ignorance on fire is better than knowledge on ice.

Legacy

noun leg·a·cy | something handed down or received from an ancestor or predecessor.

"What you leave behind is not what is engraved in stone monuments, but what is woven into the lives of others."

Pericles

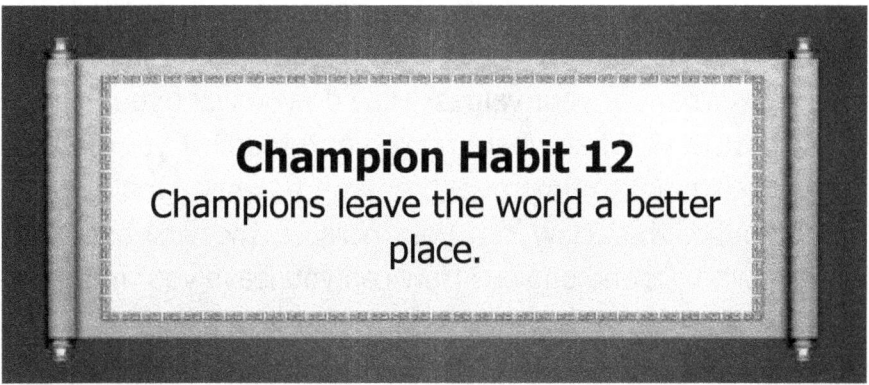

Champion Habit 12
Champions leave the world a better place.

Many spiritual teachers such as Jesus, Confucius, Lao Tzu, and Buddha have left legacies that lasted thousands of years. Many inventors have left legacies that have lasted centuries like Alexander Graham Bell and the telephone or the Wright Brothers with the airplane. Artists of all types, such as Leonardo da Vinci, also leave lasting, impactful legacies that have withstood the test of time. Some entrepreneurs and civic leaders tend to leave legacies that last decades or centuries as well.

Whether or not you realize it, you are living the legacy you will leave by the choices you make or fail to make each day. It simply depends on what type of legacy you intend to leave. So ask yourself: what do want to be remembered or known for? What do you want people to say about you after you leave this earth? Think about it.

Knowing how you want to be remembered helps you decide how to live and work today.

> *Whether or not you realize it, you are living the legacy you will leave by the choices you make or fail to make each day.*

To begin the work on your personal legacy, you must identify what matters most in life to you. What's important to you? What are your values? How do you want your life to touch others? What would make you proud? If you had to do one thing to improve the world, what would your contribution be? How can you increase the well-being of those who depend on you? How can you leave your mark on whatever you do?

> *Legacy isn't only about leaving what you've earned but also what you've learned.*

The answer to these introspective questions will help you develop a meaningful philosophy of life that goes beyond just creating financial wealth. The responses to the aforementioned questions, when answered in full truth, become the building blocks of your legacy. Knowing what's important, what drives you, and how you want to be remembered creates tremendous clarity in how you should live your life.

Legacy isn't only about leaving what you've earned but also what you've learned. We all have an opportunity to make a difference. It doesn't call for wealth, fame, or even taking giant steps—you don't have to be Oprah Winfrey or a Martin Luther King, Jr. to leave a positive mark right now, one that will linger long after you're gone. A real legacy can never be determined in terms of currency, but rather contribution.

So where can you start? Here are some pointers to inspire you. Consider the following ways to leave a legacy and then begin the work to build your own legacy today:

1. **A Legacy of Knowledge** – Everything you know is most powerful when it helps someone else. Pass your expertise, your experiences, your passions, and your excellence on to as many people as you can. Put in it in a book, speak as often as you can, and impart your wisdom to children, family, friends, and colleagues. You don't need a library or institution with your name on it to be considered important enough to teach others. We all have something inside of us that was meant to be learned by and shared with others.

2. **A Legacy of Innovation** – What can you create that leaves a mark on the world? We will remember CEOs such as Steve Jobs for a lifetime because of his legacy of some of the most impactful technology of our time. If you feel led to build something, do it. Centuries from now, the world could be using something that you spearheaded or designed.

3. **A Legacy of Positivity** – Will people say you were the reason they decided to pursue their dreams, sustain a vision, or just be happy? Every interaction you have with a person is a stamp on your legacy. Strive to be a person that uplifts

others. Motivate them. Inspire them. The world will be so much richer as a result.

4. **A Legacy of Humanity** –God created us in His image, so the greatest legacy we can leave is one that honors Him and serves others. Love more. Practice tolerance, understanding, and respect. Help where you can. Give what you can, even when you think you can't. Be kind to neighbors, strangers, and loved ones alike. When you vibrate good energy and peace, anyone you touch will never forget it.

We all want to be remembered. When we are, it indicates our lives had meaning and significance to someone other than ourselves. Learn to live and love each day as if your legacy will be determined by the day's end. Make a real effort to leave the world a better place because you were here.

A real legacy can never be determined in terms of currency, but rather contribution.

Momentum

noun mo·men·tum | force or speed of movement.

"One way to keep momentum going is to constantly have greater goals."

Michael Korda

Have you ever hesitated to take action and ended up stuck in a rut not knowing what to do? You're not alone. There are some common reasons why this happens.

Sometimes we are waiting for a sign to indicate that it's okay to move forward. We might be immobile until we feel more confident when we don't really feel up to the challenge. Or we could be thinking that if we just wait a while, those obstacles will disappear and our goals will be easier to achieve.

Okay, in some cases it's entirely possible that one of these strategies is legitimate, or at least feels like it is. But how often do we use those reasons as excuses to avoid leaving our comfort zone? Let's face it, if we are looking to justify procrastination, there is no shortage of reasonable-sounding excuses we can use.

Procrastination is the opposite of momentum! The longer we wait to take action, the harder it is to get started and build the force it takes to move upward. Circumstances will never be perfect and waiting until they are is the same as going nowhere. The truth is, it will probably never get any easier to move forward and every moment that we hold back will just make things worse.

Questioning yourself only delays the inevitable.

Momentum can't happen until we start taking action. When we avoid it, it's often because we have created resistance in our own mind. We have convinced ourselves that what we want to do is exceedingly difficult. But is that really true or is it just an avoidance technique?

Momentum is one of those rare, self-perpetuation phenomenons. That's what makes it so powerful. The perfect example of momentum is a snowball rolling down a snow-covered bank. What happens? It grows and picks up speed along the way, right? But how can you use similar power to achieve your goals and start living the life of your dreams?

Taking action leaves procrastination in the dust.

Instead of getting bogged down by excuses, try to create some momentum as soon as possible. And really, this is not something that is all that difficult to do. That giant, fast moving snowball started out small and slow. The reason it grew was because it kept moving. We don't always need to launch into action like a rocket, but we do need to start moving and to keep moving so we can build some momentum.

Taking consistent action toward your goals is the best way to build momentum. That means that taking action will get easier and easier as you go along. Eventually the actions you take will require much less effort. You'll begin to enjoy your activities because you'll feel more empowered and confident and you'll have momentum on your side.

Here are some very practical ways to start building momentum today:

1. Do one thing. Our movement and progress is often stagnant because we are attempting to take on too many new things at once. While you may have a number of ideas and changes you'd like to make, pick one and give it your all. Make it your number one target or goal.

2. Be relentless about getting it done. This is where focus is key. Building momentum demands focus and commitment to staying the course. Distractions, procrastination, and changes will come in droves once you decide to go for a goal. It's inevitable! But first things first. If your action steps include studying for thirty minutes in the morning or taking a yoga class after work, do not allow an unexpected call from a good friend or an invite to happy hour alter your schedule. Follow through on your important tasks first.

3. Don't give up too soon. Results can take time. We live in a world of immediate gratification, so hanging tough with something for an extended period of time can be challenging. Remember,

this is about building. So just continue to take a step, and then another, then another. Before you know it, you'll be where you want to be. Track your effort and worry less about tracking the results. If you do your part, you'll get to where you want to be—guaranteed.

Use momentum to overcome procrastination. Taking action leaves procrastination in the dust. If you do something every day that moves you toward your goals, you'll be too busy to think about making excuses. Consider the words of Dale Carnegie:

"Inaction breeds doubt and fear. Action breeds confidence and courage. If you want to conquer fear, do not sit home and think about it. Go out and get busy."

Now

adverb |without further delay; immediately; at once.

"Most humans are never fully present in the now, because unconsciously they believe that the next moment must be more important than this one. But then you miss your whole life, which is never not now."

Eckhart Tolle

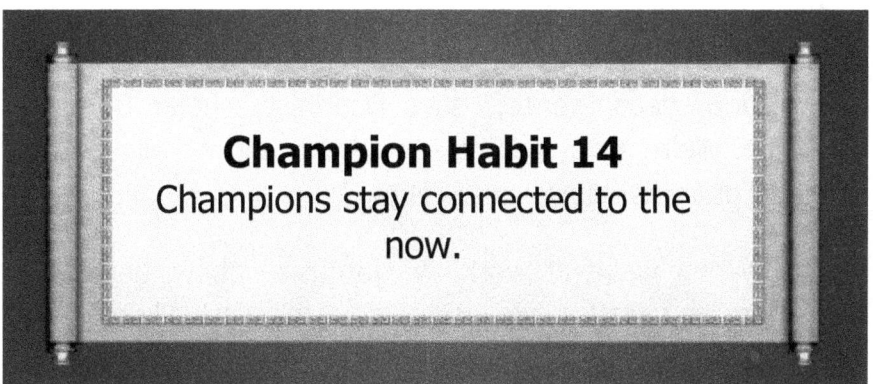

Champion Habit 14
Champions stay connected to the now.

To live in the moment, or now, means being conscious, aware, and in the present with all of your senses. It means not dwelling on the past, nor being anxious or worrying about the future.

Of course, this doesn't mean we don't need to plan, set goals, or prepare for what's to come. We can do all of these things and still enjoy each moment as it unfolds. When we train ourselves to live in the now, moment by moment and minute by minute, we immerse ourselves in that space in time and we begin to discover its beauty and wonder.

Living in the moment is not always easy. Sometimes our thoughts are overwhelmed by regrets about past events or anxiety about the future, which can make it hard to enjoy the present. We live in the age of distraction. Yet one of life's sharpest paradoxes is that your brightest future hinges on your ability to pay attention to your now.

Life unfolds in the present. But so often, we allow the present to slip away, allowing time to rush past unobserved and unseized, and squandering the precious seconds of our lives as we worry about the future and ruminate about what's past. "We're living in a world that contributes in a major way to mental fragmentation, disintegration, distraction, decoherence," says Buddhist scholar B. Alan Wallace. We're always doing something, and we allow little time to practice stillness and calm.

When we're at work, we fantasize about being on vacation; on vacation, we worry about the work piling up on our desks. We dwell on intrusive memories of the past or fret about what may or may not happen in the future.

We need to live more in the moment and learn to access the power that lies in our now experiences. Living in the moment—also called mindfulness—is a state of active, open, intentional attention on the present. When you become mindful, you realize that you are not your thoughts; you become an observer of your thoughts from moment to moment without judging them. Mindfulness involves being with your thoughts as they are, neither grasping at them nor pushing them away. Instead of letting your life go by without living it, you awaken to experience it.

Live more in the moment and learn to access the power that lies in our now experiences.

People that live in the now are happier, more exuberant, more empathetic, and more secure. They have higher self-esteem and are more accepting of their own weaknesses. Anchoring awareness in the here and now reduces the kinds of impulsivity and reactivity that underlie depression, binge eating, and attention problems. Mindful people can hear negative feedback without feeling threatened. They fight less with others and are more accommodating and less defensive. As a result, mindful people have more satisfying relationships.

Living in the now takes practice, but when you master it, you will lead a fuller life and appreciate the beauty in every activity, every second of the day. Learn how to live in the moment with these ideas:

1. Don't fast track. First, slow down. Yes, you have a lot to get done, but one step at a time. Get up early enough in the morning so you don't have to speed through your day. Take a walk or enjoy your favorite, nourishing breakfast and a cup of tea. Then jump into your day. It will all be there waiting for you. But easing into the day peacefully will keep your stress level low and help you get through the day feeling more in control and less anxious.

2. Be happy. Make an effort to smile as often as possible. Surround your environment with things you love—pictures of family or beautiful vacations, plants, candles, or music. If it makes you happy, don't save it for a special occasion. Touch happiness often.

3. Limit time spent worrying. Taking note of things that you can't control is wasted energy. It's out of your hands for a reason, so breathe, pray, and

release. Worrying means that you've left the now and moved into the future and a space of expectation. Allow God to handle what you've entrusted to Him. If you are going to pray, there is no need to worry, is it?

4. Count your blessings. You have so much to be grateful for right now. Every experience is a step closer to your destiny so see it as such. There is someone in this world who loves you to life. There is an opportunity of a lifetime waiting for you somewhere. You are reading these pages because you're alive. That means something—something significant. Take note of the simple things—the air you're breathing, the job you have now, the friends you can call on. The more grateful you are for what you have, the more goodness you will draw to you.

Since goals are future-based, living in your now should not be a goal Instead, set the intention of always paying attention to what's happening at the present moment. Become aware of being alive. As you draw your next breath, focus on the rise of your abdomen on the in-breath, and the stream of heat through your nostrils on the out-breath. If you're aware of that feeling right now, as you're reading this, you're living in the moment. Nothing happens next. It's not a destination. This is it. You're already there. Enjoy where you are on your journey right now!

Opportunity

noun op·por·tu·ni·ty | a situation or condition favorable for attainment of a goal

"A pessimist sees the difficulty in every opportunity; an optimist sees the opportunity in every difficulty."

Winston S. Churchill

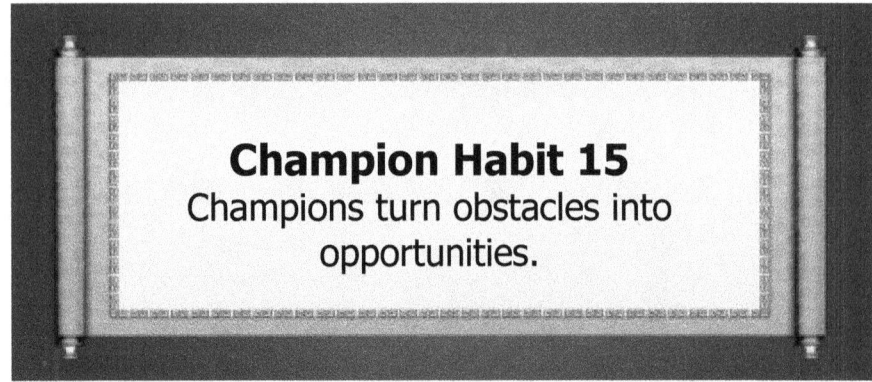

Champion Habit 15
Champions turn obstacles into opportunities.

It is impossible to seize opportunity without first seeing opportunity. Opportunity comes in all shapes, sizes, and colors and is often nestled in new experiences. Each day we are given a chance to build, to grow, to love, to create, or just to connect. More times than not, opportunity goes undetected as the masses continue to live uninspired and unaware of their greater good. There are a plethora of chances forgone each day that carry with them the power to revolutionize countless lives in remarkable ways. So the question remains, if opportunity can be so great, why is it so easy to miss? Are we too busy, too tired, or too cynical?

In the words of Thomas A. Edison, "Opportunity is missed by most people because it is dressed in overalls and looks like work."

If you have trouble seizing opportunities, you hesitate to change paths or directions in life because you have little confidence in your ability to act quickly and without deliberation. You resist change and find it difficult to be spontaneous. It is hard for you to make changes without first figuring things out from every possible direction. You know all too well that "he who hesitates is lost" and you end up having many regrets in life.

Yet you remain paralyzed as opportunities pass you by.

Seizing opportunity has both a doing side and a knowing side. The doing side is being able to seize an opportunity and take advantage of it during the time or "window of opportunity" when it is open to you. The knowing side is being able to recognize favorable circumstances when they cross your path. This helps you realize what is advantageous so you can also recognize an opportunity when you see one. You will always miss an opportunity that you cannot see. If you are good at spotting an opportunity when it exists, and how much of an opportunity is really there, then you also know when to be spontaneous and grab that opportunity. These two aspects of opportunity work together in duality. This means that as you develop the ability to recognize when an opportunity exists, you also increase the ability to seize opportunities in general.

It is impossible to seize opportunity without first seeing opportunity.

Here are some ways you can begin to see and seize more opportunity starting now:

- If you want to more opportunities, the first step is to look around you. Take a look at your life, your workplace, your community, and your social circle for ways you can make it better. Stay tuned into world events that will speak your desire to contribute to something bigger than you. If you ask the Universe for a shot, be willing to take it.

- Be open minded to new things. Opportunities don't always come in the package in which we expected, so don't shun something before you've given it some serious consideration. Be optimistic to change and give it your all. And toss away the notion of convenience—there is no such thing as a good or perfect time to go for it. If something comes your way that could be good for, make room in your life for it. Shift your schedule. Put less pressing responsibilities on the back burner or delegate them to someone else temporarily. Flexibility is key. For you to get something you've never had, you may have to do some things you've never done.

- You have to step up to the plate too. A half-hearted effort will not reap any rewards. So give every opportunity your all. Go above and beyond what's expected. Take initiative to be the best. A stellar performance will ensure that fruitful opportunities continuously come your way.

When opportunity knocks, run to the door. You never know who or what is waiting for you on the other side.

Passion

noun pas·sion | a strong or extravagant fondness, enthusiasm, or desire for anything.

"Passion is energy. Feel the power that comes from focusing on what excites you."

Oprah Winfrey

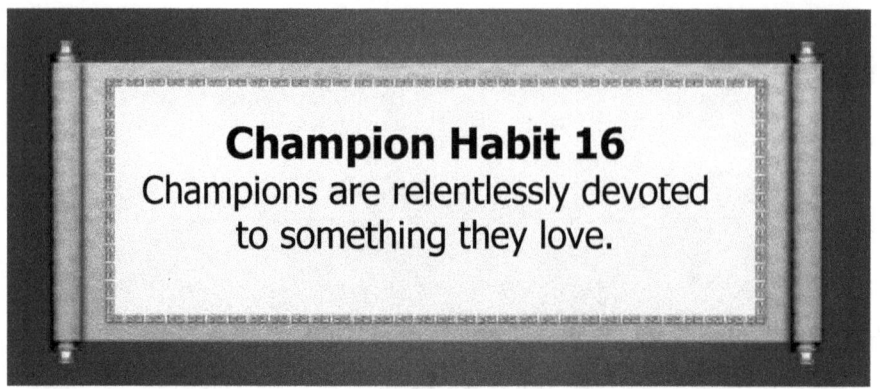

Champion Habit 16
Champions are relentlessly devoted to something they love.

Successful people win in life because they love what they do. After reading the stories of those who have gone on to make significant contributions in life, there is always a common thread of strong passion present in them all. They have passion for their field, their business, their lives. Passion is the single fastest way to spur yourself to massive success. Are you doing something you love for most of your waking hours? Something you're excited about? Something you get up early to work on or to stay up late to finish? If not, it's self-examination time.

A huge part of obtaining and maintaining a winning mentality is being able to clearly identify and articulate your areas of passion. What do you love to do? Who are you professionally? Who are you – really? What are your dreams and fears? What matters most? You have the power to create a road map from your dreams to reality. Start the transition to a new you today to achieve the results that are beyond your wildest dreams!

Find or create a working environment where you are allowed to be yourself and feel liberated to do your work as the best expression of yourself, your dreams, and your abilities. It has long been said that "What you enjoy, you do well." The crucial difference between an overachiever and an underachiever is oftentimes the level of passion, or lack thereof, that shows up in their work.

Steve Jobs, founder of Apple Computer Corporation, was one of the world's most successful entrepreneurs. On June 12, 2005, Steve Jobs gave the commencement address at Stanford University. Take a look at a few excerpts from his powerful speech that will speak to discovering your passion in life.

Find your true passion and do what you love to do. "Sometimes life hits you in the head with a brick. Don't lose faith. I'm convinced that the only thing that kept me going was that I loved what I did. You've got to find what you love. And that is as true for your work as it is for your lovers. Your work is going to fill a large part of your life, and the only way to be truly satisfied is to do what you believe is great work. And the only way to do great work is to love what you do. If you haven't found it yet, keep looking. Don't settle. As with all matters of the heart, you'll know when you find it. And, like any great relationship, it just gets better and better as the years roll on. So keep looking until you find it. Don't settle."

> *Successful people win in life because they love what they do.*

Make a difference. "When I was 17, I read a quote that went something like, "If you live each day as if it was your last, someday you'll most certainly be right." It made an impression on me, and since then, for the past 33 years, I have looked in the mirror every morning and asked myself, "If today were the last day of my life, would I want to do what I am about to do today?" And whenever the answer has been "No" for too many days in a row, I know I need to change something."

"Remembering that I'll be dead soon is the most important tool I've ever encountered to help me make the big choices in life. Because almost everything – all external expectations, all pride, all fear of embarrassment or failure – these things just fall away in the face of death, leaving only what is truly important. Remembering that you are going to die is the best way I know to avoid the trap of thinking you have something to lose. You are already naked. There is no reason not to follow your heart."

> *Your passion or natural inclinations towards things that thrill you will help you win in life.*

"Your time is limited, so don't waste it living someone else's life. Don't be trapped by dogma – which is living with the results of other people's thinking. Don't let the noise of other's opinions drown out your own inner voice. And most important, have the courage to follow your heart and intuition. They somehow already know what you truly want to become. Everything else is secondary."

Your passion or natural inclinations towards things that thrill you will help you win in life. So ask yourself, "Is this something I really enjoy doing and can sustain? What is it about my offerings that are unique or hard to find? Is this something people really want?" Make it your personal mission to thoroughly answer these questions and vow to forego sleep until you are able to do so!

Quieten

verb qui·et·en | to make quiet.

"By prevailing over all obstacles and distractions, one may unfailingly arrive at his chosen goal or destination."

Christopher Columbus

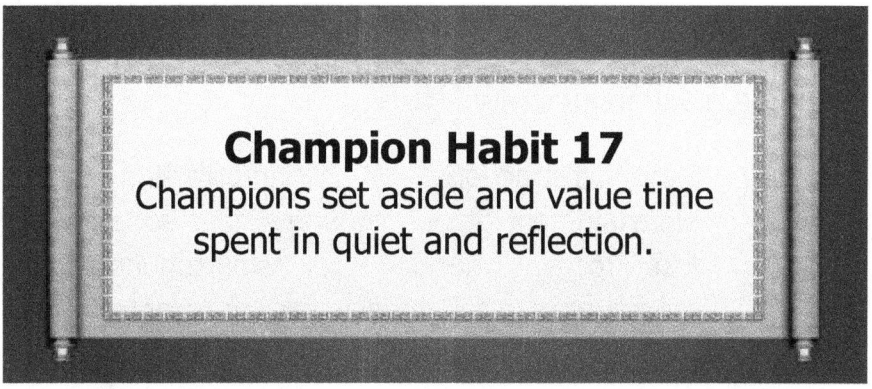

Champion Habit 17
Champions set aside and value time spent in quiet and reflection.

Our world has become a constant feed of information, noise, and entertainment. Our phones live not just in our pockets, but in front of our eyes. The influence of the Internet and its constant stream of information is accessible from nearly corner of our world. Breaking news interrupts our day at rapid speed. We are relentlessly fed messages from advertisements on nearly every flat surface. Each distraction enters our mind with one goal: Gain control of our attention and resources.

Without distractions, you can produce more and achieve at higher levels in every area of your life.

As a result, we live distracted lives and our ability to focus, create, and accomplish suffers significantly. It is increasingly clear that distractions are not going away on their own. Instead, the responsibility is ours to live attentive, intentional lives in a world filled with distraction. If we are ever to reach our full potential and have the energy to focus on what matters most in life, we must actively work each day to quieten our environments.

To live life with less distraction, consider implementing one or more of these simple habits to increase your focus and productivity:

1. Limit distractions. With information and entertainment at our fingertips, it is so easy to lose focus. Checking our smartphones for messages, social media for comments, and emails for new tasks or requests are how we feed our human desire to feel connected and productive in the world. It is not uncommon for someone to check their phone hundreds of times a day. Don't fall for the interruption trap! You are only procrastinating to avoid getting essential things done. Leave your phone out of your work space so you can resist the temptation to look at it frequently. Set aside time in your daily schedule to read the news or catch up on current or social events. Use the phone as a reward—when you get a number of things done, allow yourself 10-15 minutes of fun time before getting back to work.

2. List your tasks and goals in a planner or notebook. Seeing is believing. A tangible representation of what lies ahead each day will force your mind to be conscious of things you need to complete. It feels good to check items off as you complete them and to look back at the end of a productive day. Create a system for getting things done, such as prioritizing tasks in order of importance or tackling your biggest goals first.

3. Develop a habit of execution. Going back to maintaining momentum, get used to finishing what you start. If you set a goal to read one book a week, do it. If you decide to start a new business idea, see it through. Once your mind realizes you're serious, everything else will follow suit.

4. Know when you do your best work. Productivity is personal. We all have different internal clocks, so it's important to understand when you are most focused. If you are an early riser, take advantage of that and knock out tasks before noon. If your energy is higher at night, flip it so you work for longer periods in the evening.

5. Keep company with productive people. Iron sharpens iron, so it's critical to stay close to people who are focused and getting things done. If you don't have someone in your current circle, put out some feelers on social media or business events. Make a commitment to work in the same space at least once a week and ask for accountability if you need it.

Learning how to minimize distractions can dramatically increase your productivity and effectiveness, as well as reduce your stress. Without distractions, you can produce more and achieve at higher levels in every area of your life. Make the choice to quieten your life today so you can enjoy the life you want tomorrow.

Resilience

noun re·sil·ience | the power or ability to return to the original form, position, etc., after being bent, compressed, or stretched; elasticity.

"No industry is immune and no occupation is safe. All of us need to begin to think in terms of our own inner strengths, our resilience and resourcefulness, our capacity to adapt and to rely upon ourselves and our families."

Steven Pressfield

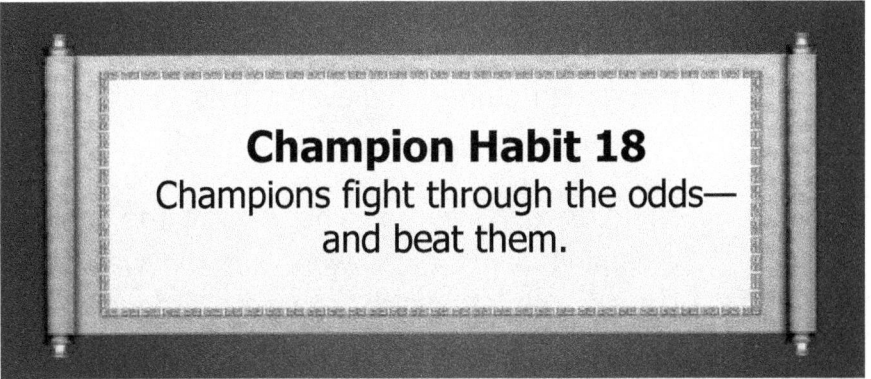

Champion Habit 18
Champions fight through the odds—
and beat them.

Resilience is the ability to push through adversity in such a way that one comes through it unscathed or even better for the experience. To be resilient means facing life's difficulties with courage and patience – refusing to give up. It is the quality of character that allows a person or group of people to rebound from misfortune, hardships, and traumas.

Resilience is rooted in a tenacity of spirit—a determination to embrace all that makes life worth living even in the face of overwhelming odds. When we have a clear sense of identity and purpose, we are more resilient, because we can hold fast to our vision of a better future.

Here are three steps for building resilience starting right now:

1. Fight for something. Your reason for doing has to be bigger than you and your personal gratification or success. What is the real reason you want whatever you're seeking? Is it for your children? For your community? For your legacy? To honor a promise you made to your parents? Ask yourself why you want it and that is your infinite source of

passion. It won't matter if something fails or doesn't work. You can pull on your passion—that inner tough stuff—whenever it gets hard. Keep your reason for greatness top of mind.

2. Fail forward. Okay, so you missed the mark. Something didn't quite work out the way you planned. You felt foolish. You were disappointed. You gave it your all and you feel like you have nothing else to give again. Guess what? You do. Failing means you tried. So dust yourself off and get back in the game. You wouldn't have a passion for what you've set out to do if it wasn't meant for you to accomplish it or find something better along the way. You're in it now. See it through. You're a champion. And champions don't quit. Ever.

3. Stay inspired. We talked about remaining focused on your big WHY, but don't underestimate the power of external motivation. Find some biographies or success stories of people you admire and read them. Pull quotes from the books and tape them up. Start a success circle with other people and cultivate a routine of sharing each other's wins. There is so much inspiration around you to keep pushing you.

Much of our resilience comes from the sense of community gained from our empowering relationships. Positive, personal connections allow us to lean on each other for support when we need it. Strive to build and maintain only those relationships that feed your drive and strengthen your resolve to win in life. You will be forced to make some tough decisions after examining your closest relationships in an effort to maintain your emotional momentum.

Don't be afraid to redefine or even refuse old alliances that no longer serve you on your quest to personal victory. Remember, you may feel alone at times so you'll need to be okay with borrowing strength from those in your corner.

> *Resilience is rooted in a tenacity of spirit—a determination to embrace all that makes life worth living even in the face of overwhelming odds.*

Even when it appears you are fighting a losing battle, know there's a crowd somewhere cheering you on. At any moment, the game can change for you—in your favor!

Surrender

verb sur·ren·der | to give oneself up, as into the power of another; submit or yield.

"Surrender to what is. Let go of what was. Have faith in what will be."

Sonia Ricotti

Champion Habit 19
A champion understands that giving in is not giving up.

There are few things more maddening than running into challenges and blockades while you're working toward an important goal. You know how it works. You'll be moving along nicely, feeling great about your progress, when all of a sudden – boom; you're stuck. You've just encountered an obstacle that you have no idea how to get around.

What you do next might determine whether you go on to achieve your goal or give up out of frustration. Our first impulse is usually to try and find a way to work through the obstacle, sidestep around it, or even force it to move out of the way.

Does that mean your goals are now toast? No, not necessarily. There's another effective option that is often overlooked when it comes to dealing with obstacles. It's called surrender. We know that when you face an obstacle, the thought of surrender can feel like you are giving up. But is that really the case? Keep in mind that the positive power of surrender is not the same as the negative power of defeat.

Surrender is a choice and our true power is always in our ability to choose. In surrender we come to a moment of judgment, where we must decide whether it is more destructive and negative or more constructive and positive to continue what we are doing. We must weigh potential gain against possible loss, and decide what best serves our purpose.

When you surrender to an obstacle as part of your success strategy, it just means that you are refusing to waste your energy fighting against it. It means that instead of resisting and struggling, you are positioning yourself so you can get a different perspective on the situation and see the obstacle in a new light.

> *When you surrender to an obstacle as part of your success strategy, it just means that you are refusing to waste your energy fighting against it.*

Just like anything else, surrendering is something you have to practice until it feels familiar to you. If you are faced with a situation that is presenting resistance, you may need to take a few steps back and re-evaluate it. Is this something that keeps coming back because you are missing the intended lesson? Are you being called to do something different or maybe stand up to it instead of playing small and running away from it? Look at the scenario from a different perspective before you decide to keep fighting against it or abandoning ship.

Once you feel that you have a good handle on the situation, listen to your spirit. Pray for the power to release into God's hands. Ask for guidance or alternatives. Keep a notebook handy as answers come to you (it could happen anywhere, so be prepared). The flow of feedback you receive may not make sense immediately, but note it anyway. The pieces will soon start to come together.

When all else seems lost, it's okay to give this thing some time. Shift your energy and focus on something else for a bit and then come back to the situation with fresh eyes and perspective. This is also a great time to recharge with something creative and fun that feeds your soul. With a renewed sense of mental and physical energy and less emotional weight, you'll feel strong enough to pick up where you left all. Sometimes surrender is just temporary.

Surrender is an attitude of being and doing our best, then giving the rest to our Higher Power, whatever we conceive that to be. Remember these key understandings as you discover the power of surrender in your own life:

- Surrender is not quitting. To quit means to stop and not go back.
- Surrender is not giving up. To give up means to stop trying.
- To give in means to yield. It is flexible, and flexibility is strength.

Thoughts

noun | ˈthôt | A single act or product of thinking; idea or notion; the product of mental activity; that which one thinks.

"We are addicted to our thoughts. We cannot change anything if we cannot change our thinking."

Santosh Kalwar

The Little Black Book for Champions

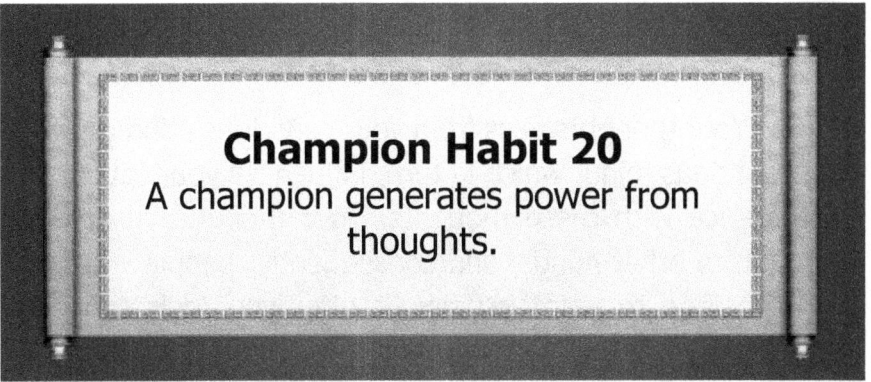

Champion Habit 20
A champion generates power from thoughts.

Your thought power is the key to creating your reality. Everything you perceive in the physical world originates in the invisible, inner domain of your thoughts and beliefs. To become the master of your destiny, you must learn to control the nature of your dominant, habitual thoughts. By doing so, you will be able to attract into your life exactly what you intend to have and experience as you come to know the truth:

Your thoughts create your reality.

If you plant seeds, water them, and fertilize them they will grow into healthy and strong plants. Thoughts, like seeds, have a natural tendency to grow and manifest in your life, if you feed them with attention, interest, and enthusiasm.

It is estimated that the average person has between 12,000 and 70,000 thoughts a day. This is evidence enough to suggest that your goal should not control every thought. You must learn to bring your dominant thoughts and beliefs under your conscious control, as they are what largely determine your mental attitude. As you do, you will find your random thoughts will become more positive and more deliberate.

Your thoughts pass from your conscious mind to your subconscious mind, which in turn, influences your actions in accordance with these thoughts. Your thoughts also pass through to other minds, and consequently, people who are in a position to help you, might offer you their support, sometimes, without even knowing why.

This might sound strange and unbelievable. Even if you are skeptical at first, if analyze the type of thoughts that come to you, and the kind of life you live, you will discover interesting things about the mind. The power of your mind is part of the creative power of the Universe, which means that your thoughts work together with it. You are a manifestation of the Universal mind.

Your subconscious mind is the storehouse of your deep-seeded beliefs. To change your circumstances and attract that which you choose, you must learn to re-program your subconscious mind. The most effective and practical way to do this is to learn the simple process of creative visualization. It is the technique underlying reality creation, using thought power to consciously imagine, create, and attract that which you choose. Your imagination is the engine of your thoughts. It converts your thought power into mental images which are in turn manifested in the physical realm.

Here you will find some key understandings that will guide you in maximizing your own thought power:

- **Thoughts are warning signs.** Treat them as such. When become initially conscious of our thoughts, it's tempting for the negative stuff to stand out. All of sudden, you'll become aware of every fearful, harsh, critical idea that pops into your mind. Instead of investing energy in analyzing them, just dismiss counterproductive thoughts. They creep in to challenge your commitment and our focus. Strike them done and refuse to give them power. If you see danger headed your way, do you swerve the car or head right into the construction zone? Handle your thought life the same way. When you sense negativity coming, shift in the direction of positivity.

- **Replace Negative With Positive.** Maintain a mental rolodex of positive thoughts that you can flip through at a moment's notice. As soon as an "I can't" doubt-filled statement comes to mind, counteract it with, "This is mine. I'm claiming it." Practice swapping negative thoughts with positive ones until it becomes second nature.

Your life is the perfect mirror of your thoughts, beliefs, and dominant mental attitude. Whether you realize it or not, you are already creating your reality through your thought power. Every effect you see in your outside world was originally caused within you—no exceptions.

Watch your thoughts, they become words. Watch your words, they become actions. Watch your actions, they become habits. Watch your habits, they become your character. Watch your character—it becomes your destiny.

Watch your thoughts, they become words. Watch your words, they become actions. Watch your actions, they become habits. Watch your habits, they become your character. Watch your character—it becomes your destiny.

Universe

noun uni·verse | a world or sphere in which something exists or prevails; the whole world, especially with reference to humanity.

"The universe doesn't give you what you ask for with your thoughts - it gives you what you demand with your actions."

Steve Maraboli

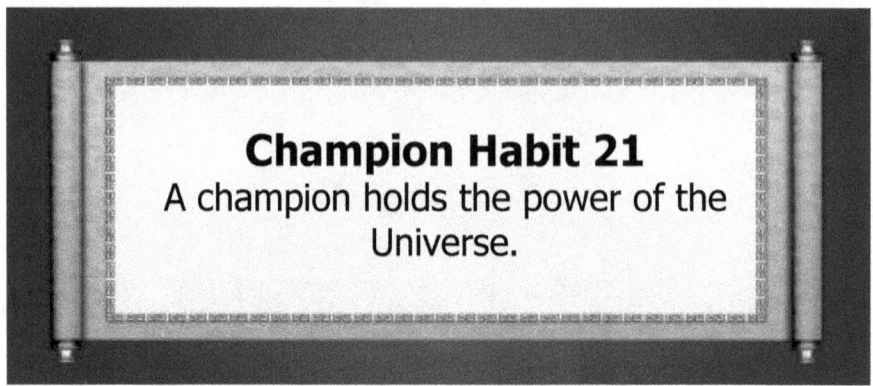

Champion Habit 21
A champion holds the power of the Universe.

Do you know who and what you are? Do you know your role in this Universe?

How often do you think about the world in which you live? Not politics or the economy, but the power of the Universe – the vastness of the sky, the depths of the ocean, the richness of the earth, the diversity in nature, and you as a sentient participant?

The Universe is everything we can touch, feel, sense, measure, or detect. It includes living things, planets, stars, galaxies, dust clouds, light, and even time. Before the birth of the Universe, time, space, and matter did not exist.

We are one with the Universe. We are the Universe and the Universe is within us. To harness the power of the Universe is to command and demand that it does what we wish for it to do. That is the secret to life, the Law of Attraction.

Imagine a world where we can attract what we desire simply by manifesting that idea or thought in our minds. Imagine having the ability to control our own Universe; to truly live the lives we've always dreamed of. Well, that isn't your imagination—it's happening right now. This is no lie, trick, or hoax; it is simply the manipulation of how the universe operates.

Without being consciously aware of it, you have been secretly using the power of the Universe and the Law of Attraction. However, it has been used in a way that has been non-beneficial to our lives. Well, today will be the day you'll be able to fully grasp, understand, utilize, and harness the power of the Universe.

> *Your clear vision is your seed. Choose it wisely and precisely, and riches beyond your imagination in every area of your life shall be yours.*

You can easily begin to tap into your Universal power. Start with claiming what you want before you have it or even have a plan to get it. If you want financial abundance, start to think wealthy thoughts. See yourself investing, living in your dream home, walking your children into the best school in the area. Feel it deep in your soul; let the vision envelop you. Think about it every single day—in fact multiple times a day. Make it a part of you until it manifests.

Next, write your vision down and make it a daily affirmation. Begin each day with, "I will..." and complete the statement with your goal. Repeat the statement at least 15 times in a row. Keep it posted on a mirror, in your car, in front of your desk—any place where you'll see it frequently. You want your mind and spirit to align and believe that your desires are unquestionably possible.

Refuse to spend anytime dwelling on what could happen. We have a tendency to speed up the future and start to focus on everything that could go wrong as opposed to what could go right. If you want to launch a new business, don't focus on becoming overloaded with orders before you get the first one in the door.

And most importantly, act! Nothing good can happen for you until you transform thought into action. You won't know until you try so start right now. Just do the work.

Here's the thing. The Universe will only deliver to you that which is rightfully yours and that which you have the capacity to receive. If you find it seemingly impossible to manifest in your life, just know you might be looking for something that is simply not yours or that you are not yet ready to handle. If you find yourself here, submit to a process of true self-reflection to determine your reason for delay.

Begin to harness the power of the Universe and see a positive change in your life today! Remember, anyone can do it at any time. However, failure to complete all of the steps above may prevent the Law of Attraction from functioning properly in your life. Practice the following affirmation to help you harness your power daily.

AFFIRMATION:

Today, I tap into the power of the Universe.

The Universe offers unlimited possibilities to us all. This abundance of this world is within my reach because I am one with this force. I am open as a conduit for this power to flow through me. As I consciously direct my thoughts and energy, I manifest my desired reality. I am an active participant in the creation and evolution of my daily life and the world around me.

Today, I tap into the power of the Universe.

Vision

noun vi·sion | the act or power of anticipating that which will or may come to be; an experience in which a personage, thing, or event appears vividly or credibly to the mind, although not actually present, often under the influence of a divine or other agency.

"The only thing worse than being blind is having sight but no vision."

Helen Keller

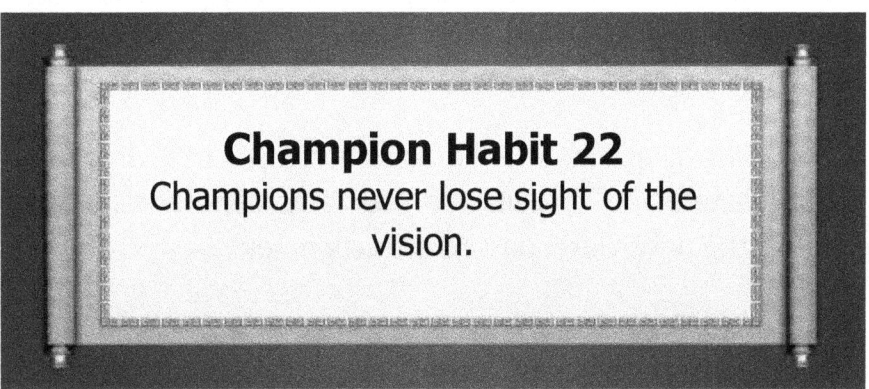

Champion Habit 22
Champions never lose sight of the vision.

Without a clear and precise vision of exactly what you want, you'll never reach it or have it. Whatever we focus on and emotionalize often is what we will attract and actually see in the quantum field of all possibilities, or better yet, probabilities.

As unconventional as this may sound, this theory is now being proven in the world of quantum physics, leaving no shadow of a doubt that it's true. What does this mean for you? That the more clearly focused you are on exactly what you want, the easier and faster you'll manifest everything you need to make it a physical reality.

Since all material things move from the non-physical to the physical reality, our vision and goals are paramount in the process of achievement. Our vision and focus act like a magnet that attracts and connects the pieces together.

Keep in mind that the Universe operates by natural laws, exact precision, and perfect order. Our vision, then, must also be precise and exact in our mind in order for whatever we need to be attracted and shown to us by the intelligent forces that govern all of creation. When we focus our brain on what we want, we actually increase the amplitude of the cellular vibration and cause the "attraction" factor to really take shape.

Just like a magnifying glass can focus the sun's rays and create a fire, focusing on your vision and goals keeps you in the right vibration and attraction field.

When we choose a vision or goal that is bigger than our current reality, we are in essence creating a gap or a vacuum between what we want and where we currently are. We know from natural law that nature fills a void or gap in the fastest and most efficient ways possible.

There is a body of research that proves when we're fully engaged and emotionalized in our clear vision, we emit a frequency from our brain and heart that penetrates and permeates all space and time, and brings forth to us everything that's in resonance with the image we're holding.

The frequency we emit is our personal electromagnetic frequency. Just like a radio station that sends out a signal, we release our own energy based on our dominating thoughts at a conscious and subconscious level.

Just imagine how an apple seed attracts the nutrients it needs from the soil to grow its roots, and then once it sprouts above the ground, the sun adds its magic and food through photosynthesis. Then, low and behold, the seed becomes an apple tree.

> *We have the ability to, either knowingly or unknowingly, direct the wind in our life with our words.*

You too will attract exactly what you need to realize your dreams when you really start to believe and feel your vision becoming a reality. It's the clear and consistent vibration of your vision that brings forth your needs. You provide the seed; the Universe provides the resources.

Therefore, you must now make your "new vision" inside of your brain more real than the current results in your outside world. Then, and only then, will the Universe begin to present its riches to you in the most convenient and efficient ways possible.

Your clear vision is your seed. Choose it wisely and precisely, and riches beyond your imagination in every area of your life shall be yours.

Visualization is the first step to bringing a dream to life. If you can see yourself happy, successful, healthy, and loving life, you can make it happen. The first step is to visualize it. In order to create and inspire a winning vision, you must engage in the following steps daily: 1) See yourself the way you want to be, 2) Strive to understand why you exist, and 3) Define and stay true to your deep values.

Take a few minutes right now to achieve your goals in your mind. Imagine a life that is exactly as you want it.

What would you do each day? Who would you do it with? Nothing is too crazy or ambitious. A few seconds is all it takes to put you in a state of excitement and enthusiasm. If you can see your goal in your mind, you can make it a reality!

Never underestimate the power of vision.

Words

noun | a unit of language, consisting of one or more spoken sounds or their written representation, that functions as a principal carrier of meaning.

"Words are singularly the most powerful force available to humanity. We can choose to use this force constructively with words of encouragement, or destructively using words of despair. Words have energy and power with the ability to help, to heal, to hinder, to hurt, to harm, to humiliate and to humble."

Yehuda Berg

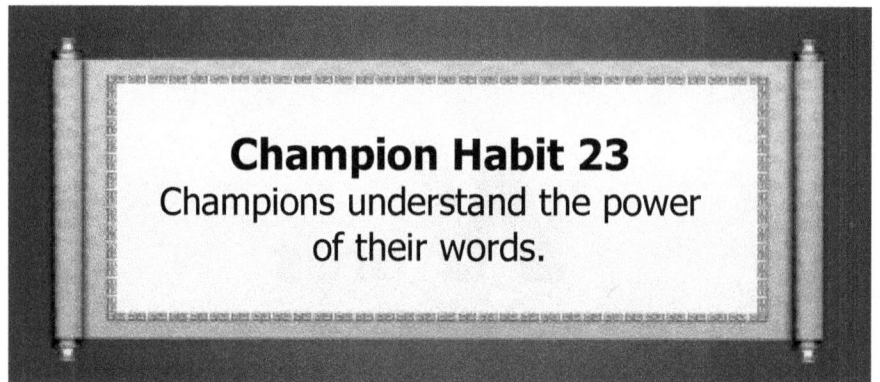

Champion Habit 23
Champions understand the power of their words.

Words have incredible power in our lives. They provide us with a vehicle for expressing and sharing our experiences with others. Everything we say, or think, has the potential to either heal or harm. Our words can destruct or construct, be positive or negative. Whatever choice we make, to harm or heal, it is never the words themselves that directly cause the outcome. Words simply are. It is how we use them, and what we bring or associate with them, that creates the end result.

Because the words we speak either aloud, or in the privacy of our minds, embody our intentions, they are a carrier of our energy. Our words represent us. And as you know, we can have good, bad, or indifferent word moments or even days.

Most of us don't realize, however, that the words we habitually choose also affect what we experience. The reality is you can transform your life by transforming your vocabulary. Transformational Vocabulary is about how you can take control of your habitual vocabulary to change the quality of your life. By simply changing your habitual vocabulary—the words you consistently use to describe the emotions of your life—you can instantly change how you think, feel, and how you live.

Using transformational vocabulary, as taught by self-help guru Tony Robbins, can help you to change your thoughts and your outlook. Changing your outlook can have a huge impact on the results you experience.

Here are four tips for obtaining transforming results by using transforming vocabulary:

1. **Look at those life situations that are causing you stress or attracting unwanted results.**

   Ask yourself: How am I viewing this situation? Are my thoughts empowering? Empowering thoughts and words open you up to what's possible.

2. **Replace limiting words with words that give life.**

   "Should, Must, and Have To" become "Could, Want, and Choose To."

3. **Do the words you use fit the scenario?**

   Calmer words lead to a more peaceful state of mind. Likewise, words that are passionate will fire you up. Learn to choose the words that fuel the emptions you need to feel in the moment.

4. **Watch out for limiting language and black and white thinking.**

Avoid phrases like there is no point, it never works, you always…

5. **Ask people you trust to give you feedback on the language you use most frequently.**

Someone who is honest will tell you if you speak more negatively than positively. If there input is more constructive that you expected, it's okay. You need an outside perspective so you change for the better.

> *We have the ability to, either knowingly or unknowingly, direct the wind in our life with our words.*

As individuals, we may be powerless to change the world—but we can change ourselves. We can only impact the world when we learn to change our world. We can make a choice to pass on negativity or positivity in our speech. Our words do matter. They are powerful. We have the ability to, either knowingly or unknowingly, direct the wind in our life with our words.

Pay attention to how you use your words.

X-ray

noun | A photograph or image obtained through the use of x-rays.

"Don't become preoccupied with what is happening around you. Pay more attention to what is going on within you."

Mary Frances Winters

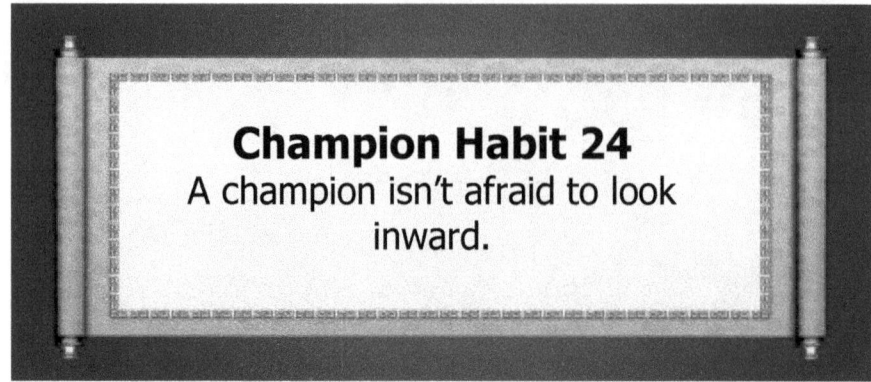

Champion Habit 24
A champion isn't afraid to look inward.

An X-ray is a common imaging test that has been used for decades to help doctors view the inside of the body without having to make an incision. Through the images generated in X-rays, physicians are able to closely examine internal structures such as bones and organs to determine the extent of an injury or even diagnose a disease. The power of this modern-day technology has saved countless lives simply by looking inside the body to determine the source of outwardly manifested pain and discomfort.

Let's think for a moment about the use of x-rays in a more figurative sense. Imagine if x-rays could be used to determine the real cause of your unhappiness, limited thinking, feeling stuck, and poor self-perceptions. What might the light reveal by taking a deeper look at your fears and inhibitions? What do you really think about the person staring back at you each day in the mirror? While this level of vulnerability and transparency is foreign to the masses, a huge part of building a champion's mentality is embracing the power of introspection.

Introspection is defined as an inward look into one's own thoughts and feelings; the process of self-examination.

While it has become second nature to think critically about people and things around us, the ironic part is we often forget to apply this concept to ourselves. In a society fixated on fast-paced environments and a "microwave" mentality, it's difficult to find the time to sit down and reflect. However, setting aside a small portion of your day for self-examination can be a lot more helpful than you might expect.

Self-analysis and reflection can be positive tools in your daily life, so don't resist being alone with your thoughts. When you are still and examining your life from a different point of you, you'll notice things that weren't obvious before. There may be relationships that need to end and boundaries that have to be strengthened. But if you resist taking the time to reflect, you'll miss everything that is demanding your immediate attention. Most importantly, you'll remain stuck in fear.

Let's consider this. The reason we hide from ourselves is because we want to avoid the truth. Instead of standing in front of their mirror and taking a good hard look at ourselves and our stuff, we'd rather duck around in the dark. But

When trouble, mishaps, or hiccups arise along the way, either real or perceived, be sure to reach for your mirror to engage in immediate self-examination.

when you finally face it, you can address it. You can shift gears to get a different result. You can let go of what you can't change and figure out what you can. But you can't do any of that until you get up close and personal with it.

It's possible that you've been scarred by some failures, missteps, or rejection that have made you want to bury your head in the sand rather than get to the root of it. The key is figure out what lies beneath everything that is holding you back so you create a sense of awareness. What the sources of your pain? (And go as far back as you need to with this.) Who told you that you couldn't do something? Who questioned your gifts and discounted your dreams? What experiences in life fed your fear instead of your faith? Can you see why it would be important to know? You guessed it. So you can clear your life of those people and their negative thoughts. If you don't, you'll continue to reopen wounds that need to heal, but never have a chance to do so. Repeat this self-reflection exercise until you have clarity.

When you seek answers from within, you strengthen trust in your own voice. Often, too much input only clouds your judgement and confuses you. Instead, learning how to rely on your own ideas and conscience, you will soon find that you are tuning out the noise. You'll fortify your confidence. You'll become your loudest cheerleader. You will seek advice from the only person who really counts—you.

Going inward is how you find the solutions you may be desperately seeking elsewhere. You can take inventory of what needs to go and what needs to stay. The people, the places, the experiences that bring you the most joy? Keep those. The people, places (like a job that you'll miserable and unaccomplished in), and experiences that you dread? Cut those. It may seem like a daunting task, and, in some cases, it will be. However, this exercise is critically necessary to your elevation and transformation.

Spending as little as five to ten minutes a day can begin the process of making introspection second nature. When trouble, mishaps, or hiccups arise along the way, either real or perceived, be sure to reach for your mirror to engage in immediate self-examination. It is the first place, and really the only place, where real revelation and change happens. Just like an x-ray reveals what is happening beneath the surface when we experience pain, true introspection will lead us to the causes of our inner misalignment. Equipped with that truth, we are better able to move forward in life, in most cases, effortlessly.

Yes

noun | - an affirmative reply.

"I say "YES" to the opportunities life offers me."

Jonathan Lockwood Huie

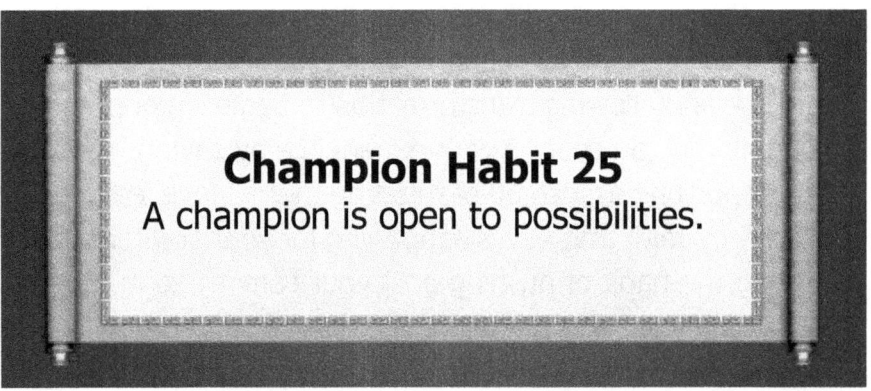

Champion Habit 25
A champion is open to possibilities.

How many times have you said "no" to something you really wanted to do? Does indecision or fear hold you back? What could you experience if you simply said "yes"?

In the words of Napoleon Bonaparte, "Take time to deliberate, but when the time for action has arrived, stop thinking and go in." You won't always have all of the information, and the circumstances may not appear to be just right. However, at a certain point you simply have to say "yes." If the situation doesn't work out the way you hoped, you will still learn. Planning is good, but until you take action nothing will happen. Waiting for things to be "perfect" is a form of procrastination. In fact, indecision can be debilitating. It is a passive choice with often regretful consequences. It often leads to a habit of vacillating – always being in limbo. In that mode, you will never achieve your dreams, or at the very least, you will lose momentum and delay positive results. In the words of Margaret Thatcher, "Standing in the middle of the road is very dangerous; you get knocked down by the traffic from both sides."

Saying "yes" with conviction breeds an affirmative mindset. It's a way of opening up to the power of the Universe and allowing transformation to begin. In one single moment you can change your experience by saying "yes" to life's opportunities instead of resisting them. Move fear aside and rely on faith that ALL is happening for your greater good. Get into the habit of pushing past your comfort zone. If you don't think you have the courage, then borrow some!

> *Follow your intuition and see where it takes you.*

If you want to win in life, then develop a "yes" mentality. Say "yes" and sample a new food. Say "yes" and explore a new relationship. Say "yes" and accept a new job assignment. Follow your intuition and see where it takes you. It's been said that the power of "yes" is a measure of your soul. As you add more "yes" into your life, remember to focus your energy. Always keep your overarching vision in mind, making value-driven decisions. In this way, each "yes" will lead you closer to fulfilling your divine destiny. Here are some action steps you can start taking today to unleash the power of "yes" in your life:

- Make "yes" a habit. Comfort tells us to say "no" more than we say "yes." Before you turn down the chance to do something unfamiliar, hear the person out. Get the details. Do some research. And put your fear aside and see how the idea feels. If your spirit says do it, follow that intuition. If things don't work out, you're not completely stuck. You can change your mind for the right reasons (other than just wanting to quit). So start saying "yes" a little more often and watch the positive results unfold.

- Switch it up. Say "yes" to something new today. Do you always do the same sandwich shop for lunch alone? Accept a colleague's invitation to have sushi with the group. Try a new route to your office or a different hair color. These may seem like little things, but they have a significant impact on shifting your willingness to be open and welcoming the power of affirmative behavior.

- Become the person you wish to be. To be different, you have to act the part. You have the power to change your persona and behavior today, so do it! Want to be a more powerful speaker? Get in front of mirror and practice or record yourself rehearsing. Send it to someone for positive feedback and adjust accordingly. Next step? Get in front of an audience of strangers and test it out. You can become anyone you want to be—the gifts are already planted inside of you. Use them!

AFFIRMATION:

Today, I say "yes" to life!

When I say "yes," life responds. I have faith in the power of the Universe. I do not make excuses out of fear. I simply have to claim my Good. I battle fear with faith. I honor inspirations through action. I move past the status quo. I seek new experiences and everyday joys. I understand that even if I fall, I will pick up knowledge that stays with me forever. Today, I say "yes" to life!

Zeal

noun | ˈzēl\fervor for a person, cause, or object; eager desire or endeavor; enthusiastic diligence; ardor.

"Zealous men are ever displaying to you the strength of their belief, while judicious men are showing you the grounds of it."

William Shenstone

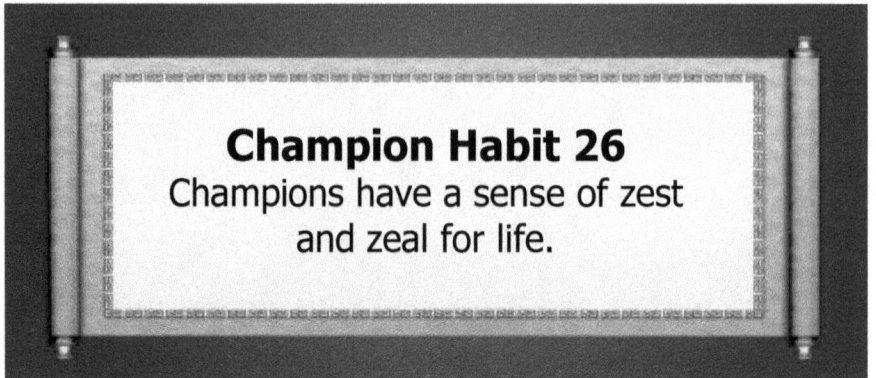

Champion Habit 26
Champions have a sense of zest and zeal for life.

The spiritual practice of zeal means being fully aroused by life. We tap into this divine energy that pulsates within us and around us by living in the present. Zealous people are ready for anything that comes their way and see every moment as a golden gateway to new possibilities.

This spiritual practice includes a wholehearted delight in the senses and a passionate love for who we are and what we have been given. In our pursuit of passion in our lives, we are encouraged by our companions on the path and the countless teachers who stretch our souls. Our zeal moves us to live compassionately and to serve others. It shows up in our prayers, rituals, family life, and community activities.

Zeal is the last principle in this book and appropriately so as it incorporates many of those that have come before it. Zeal means living abundantly — to remain in the present, have gratitude, and constantly experience wonder.

Our zeal is an energetic and committed response to opportunities and challenges that come our way.

That is much more likely when we have regular practices of devotion, are committed to integrity, have a faith relationship with our Higher Power, and view life as what it truly is— a quest that will ultimately lead us to our destiny and our higher calling. Our only responsibility is to move toward it.

> *Zeal is the essence of a truly meaningful life.*

Have you ever felt like life is passing you by? Invite zeal in and welcome all that comes your way. Greet every idea, every dream, and every desire, with an open and full heart. Zeal is a direct reflection of your inner power and state of joy, so radiate life. Be hungry for life and success. Look forward and not backward. And always be willing to reset.

Here are some ways to hang on to your zealous spirit when life becomes too crowded and noisy:

Stay in constant create mode. When you're open, you become an endless flow of new ideas. Get into creative spaces often—outdoors, in art galleries, museums, bookstores—anywhere you are surrounded by ideas, sounds, and stimulation. You'll find something exciting at every turn. Write them down and decide what to explore now and what to save for later.

Stay patient. A sense of anticipation feeds positivity. If you allow yourself to become too anxious, you may miss critical steps. While you don't want to move so slowly that your momentum dissipates, trust the timing and pacing of things in your life. If you're showing up, you're fine. Everything else will fall into place.

Stay in peace. Along those same lines as avoiding anxiety, hold your peace. Check in with yourself regularly and listen to your inner power voice in prayer or meditation. Bring your desires to mind and sit still with them. Let the warmth of realized dreams wash over you. Do this at least once a day to prepare your spirit for positive things to come.

Living a life full of zeal is what each of us should aspire to and ultimately achieve. Zeal is the essence of a truly meaningful life. We are in a constant state of evolution and change is constant. Remember life is a journey—one meant to explore and embrace. Enjoy it. Never look back. Remain excited about your future.

And be willing to allow life to create the incredible opportunities you desire and deserve.

Today is your day—greet it with enthusiasm. Follow your path with passion. Seize every second to walk towards greatness that awaits you.

Conclusion

You Are a Champion!

Are you ready to claim your destiny? To be the winner, the overcomer, the conqueror you are called to be? To rise up and raise up to something higher—something bigger—than you ever imagined possible? To design a life that you love and one that makes a mark on the world that is so extraordinary it cannot be erased?

This is your time. There has been something stirring inside of you to push harder than you ever have before. It's what you've always desired to do, to be more, and to be great. This is your destiny. Now you have the knowledge to make your dreams into realities. But remember, knowledge alone is not enough. You have to turn that knowledge into action. That is where the power lies.

Remind yourself of the habits and principles in this book and come back to them often as your daily dose of encouragement, inspiration, and motivation. Every time you feel self-doubt or fear attempting to rear its ugly head, turn up the volume on your power voice and drown out the negative noise. You can do this. You are more ready than you know.

Today is the day that you free yourself from limitations and from any ideals, labels, or naysayers all holding you back. Today is the day that you define success for yourself and decide what it looks and feels like to you.

Today is the day that you transform your life.

We want you to begin to believe in the power of possibility. Look around you. There is nothing you that desire that is out of your reach. You can master something so that other people will stand in line to pay you for it. You can have a life that you love. You can stop being complacent and be courageous enough to get what you want—and what you deserve.

Begin to speak to the champion inside of you. See yourself as a winner. Put your blinders on and block the haters and hecklers around you. Make a decision that what you want in life is worth fighting for. Vow to play and strategically plan for victory. It won't be easy, but know it is possible. Remember, having the courage to create the rich, abundant life of your dreams, not the number of successes or setbacks, is what makes you a champion.

Will this journey have a few bumps in the road? Sure. But anything worth having is worth fighting for. Release yourself from the expectations that things will be smooth, perfect, or easy. Instead, focus your energy on what is abundantly possible for you. Put everything you have into getting what the Universe has for you—that which only belongs to you. And you don't have to do this alone. Find positive people who can support you along the way. Join our movement at www.TransformYourLifeMastermind.net.

Hello, Champion. The world has been waiting for you.

Chapter 1

When you give unselfishly, your life will be enriched in unimaginable ways.

Focus on the little things that can make a meaningful difference in someone's life today.

Chapter 2

It is your belief that gives you strength and endurance beyond what you thought you were capable of.

Your beliefs should never go down without a fight.

Chapter 3

It takes courage to wade out into the deep waters of your destiny.

Rejecting the small and narrow path and opening your mindset to new, broader spaces of greatness requires courage.

There will be times when you are the only courageous soul in a room overflowing with cowards who are too afraid to take a chance on themselves or have an opinion contrary to the masses. Get comfortable with that.

Chapter 4
Your tomorrow rests in the hands of your choices.

Be decisive and flex your decision-making muscles often.

Chapter 5
Learn to live an existence filled with possibilities rather than expectations.

Until you are enlightened, you will repeatedly fall into expectations instead of leaning into possibilities.

Chapter 6
You can do whatever you set out to do— if you make up your mind that it's achievable.

Mental toughness comes simply from the decision to show up consistently and do the work.

Chapter 7
You have to do more than want it; you have to go after it.

The people you surround yourself with feed you, spiritually and mentally. They will either drive you or drown you—the decision is yours.

Chapter 8
To choose to not honor your word is to choose not to have integrity in your life.

Chapter 9

No action, gesture, or conversation is too small when it comes to how others perceive you.

Chapter 10
A joyful, peaceful, and fulfilling life is your God-given birthright!

Chapter 11
Action, not knowledge, is power.

Ignorance on fire is better than knowledge on ice.

Chapter 12
Whether or not you realize it, you are living the legacy you will leave by the choices you make or fail to make each day.

Legacy isn't only about leaving what you've earned but also what you've learned.

A real legacy can never be determined in terms of currency, but rather contribution.

Chapter 13
Taking action leaves procrastination in the dust.

Chapter 14
Live more in the moment and learn to access the power that lies in our now experiences.

Chapter 15
It is impossible to seize opportunity without first seeing opportunity.

Chapter 16

Successful people win in life because they love what they do.

Your passion or natural inclinations towards things that thrill you will help you win in life.

Chapter 17
Without distractions, you can produce more and achieve at higher levels in every area of your life.

Chapter 18
Resilience is rooted in a tenacity of spirit—a determination to embrace all that makes life worth living even in the face of overwhelming odds.

Don't be afraid to redefine or even refuse old alliances that no longer serve you on your quest to personal victory.

Chapter 19
When you surrender to an obstacle as part of your success strategy, it just means that you are refusing to waste your energy fighting against it.

Chapter 20
Watch your thoughts, they become words. Watch your words, they become actions. Watch your actions, they become habits. Watch your habits, they become your character. Watch your character—it becomes your destiny.

Chapter 21
The Universe is ready and willing to deliver unto you that which you have the capacity and belief to receive.

Chapter 22
Your clear vision is your seed. Choose it wisely and precisely, and riches beyond your imagination in every area of your life shall be yours.

Chapter 23
We have the ability to, either knowingly or unknowingly, direct the wind in our life with our words.

Chapter 24
When trouble, mishaps, or hiccups arise along the way, either real or perceived, be sure to reach for your mirror to engage in immediate self-examination.

Chapter 25
Follow your intuition and see where it takes you.

Chapter 26
Zeal is the essence of a truly meaningful life.

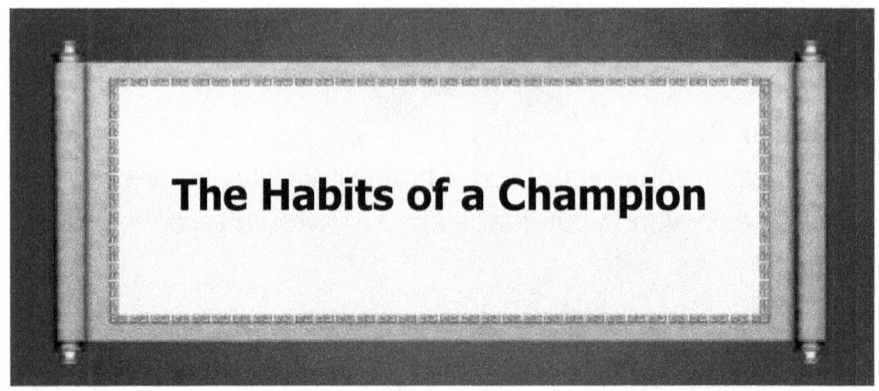

The Habits of a Champion

Champion Habit 1: A champion is always kind, generous, and compassionate towards others.

Champion Habit 2: A champion believes in believing.

Champion Habit 3: A champion displays courage in the face of fear.

Champion Habit 4: A champion is decisive.

Champion Habit 5: A champion seeks—and finds—good and greatness.

Champion Habit 6: A champion holds firm and doesn't flinch regardless of the size of the lion roaring in front of them.

Champion Habit 7: A champion knows that growth breeds success.

Champion Habit 8: Champions live in integrity.

Champion Habit 9: A champion leaves a mark.

Champion Habit 10: A champion seeks and speaks joy.

Champion Habit 11: Champions learn while living and apply while doing.

Champion Habit 12: Champions leave the world a better place.

Champion Habit 13: A champion maintains movement and momentum, never stopping or stalling.

Champion Habit 14: Champions stay connected to the now.

Champion Habit 15: Champions turn obstacles into opportunities.

Champion Habit 16: Champions are relentlessly devoted to something they love.

Champion Habit 17: Champions set aside and value time spent in quiet and reflection.

Champion Habit 18: Champions fight through the odds—and beat them.

Champion Habit 19: A champion understands that giving in is not giving up.

Champion Habit 20: A champion generates power from thoughts.

Champion Habit 21: A champion holds the power of the Universe.

Champion Habit 22: Champions never lose sight of the vision.

Champion Habit 23: Champions understand the power of their words.

Champion Habit 24: A champion isn't afraid to look inward.

Champion Habit 25: A champion is open to possibilities.

Champion Habit 26: Champions have a sense of zest and zeal for life.

References

"How to Start a Conversation With a Potential Romantic Partner." Our Everyday Life. N.p., n.d. Web. 04 Nov. 2016.

"10 First Impressions That Matter." Little Things Matter. N.p., n.d. Web. 04 Nov. 2016.

"Passion: THE POWER OF PASSION. Do What You Love To Do - the Key to Your Achievements and Success." Passion: THE POWER OF PASSION. Do What You Love To Do - the Key to Your Achievements and Success. N.p., n.d. Web. 04 Nov. 2016.

"Say What Your Mean - Using Transformational Vocabulary to Get What You Want - PMC Training." PMC Training. N.p., n.d. Web. 04 Nov. 2016.